AMAZON FIRE MAX 11 USER GUIDE (2022)

Detailed Instructions with Illustrations on How to Setup & Use the fire max 11th generation tablet, (Alexa manual) With Tips and Tricks for Beginners and Seniors

SCOTT WHETZEL

All rights reserved.

Copyright (C) 2023 Scott Whetzel.

No section of this book may be duplicated or used in any way without the Publisher's/writer's express consent.

DISCLAIMER

This book provides a plethora of information, all of which is provided in good faith and for general knowledge only.

You can learn a lot of facts and details by following the illustrations and step-by-step instructions in this book. We make every attempt to only provide high-quality content, but we cannot be held liable for any losses or harm that may arise from using this book.

Please be aware that the images and visuals in this book are only being utilized for editorial and instructional purposes.

Table of Contents

FIRE MAX 11 fEATURES 1

INTRODUCTION 2

CHAPTER 1 4

Getting started 4

    Putting a Sim card in a fire max 11 tablet 4

Setting up your fire max gadget 5

    Forgot to set up a password when setting Up My Fire Tablet? 9

CHAPTER 2 10

Connecting your Fire Max 11 tablet to the Internet 10

    Method 1: linking or pairing to an accessible Wi-Fi service ... 10

    Manually Adding a Wi-Fi Network in Method 2 13

CHAPTER 3 14

Making Calls and receiving a call 14

    Using a Fire tablet to make a video call 14

        To begin a video call from a Fire tablet 15

CHAPTER 4 16

Texting and mailing messages on your Fire max 11 16

    Configure Your Fire Tablet for Email 16

    Receiving Emails on your Fire Max 11 gadget 16

    Getting SMS and MMS Messages on a Fire 11 gadget 17

CHAPTER 5 19

How to Use an Amazon Fire Tablet as a New or Experienced User 19

    Instructions for Using & Navigating the Fire Interface 20

Adding Applications to your fire max tablet 23

Utilizing the new fire max Web Browser 25

CHAPTER 6 28

Rebooting the iPad 28

Delete or clean out all app data 28

CHAPTER 7 30

Storage and SD cards 30

Inserting and removing sd card 30

How to Store Data on an SD Card Using a Fire Tablet 32

Using an SD Card with a Fire Tablet for Portable Storage .. 32

Utilizing SD Cards as Internal Storage and formatting your card 35

Utilize these procedures to transfer applications to your SD card: 37

Expanding your storage space 38

Format your storage 39

CHAPTER 8 40

Wireless Keyboard, Detachable Case with stylus pen 40

Install your device 40

Remove your device 40

Detaching your gadget's keyboard 41

Put the keyboard in Sleep Mode 42

Charging your keyboard 42

Synchronizing a Bluetooth keyboard with your device 43

CHAPTER 9 46

Using Alexa on your new Fire Tablet 46

How to Make Alexa Work (activate) on Your Fire Tablet.......46
Utilizing Alexa with your Fire tablet..47
Installing Alexa on your new fire max gadget.......................49
Steps to set Alexa up on your Fire tablet................................49
Utilizing Touch to call Alexa on your new Fire Tab 49
Use your Fire tablet's Alexa hands-free mode......................51
    Setting fire max 11 Show Mode Charging Dock up............51
Utilize the Show Mode Charging Dock....................................52
Toggle your fire max gadget to show the mode 53
    Activate show mode on your gadget 53
    Turn off or disable show mode on your device 53
Read Kindle Books via Alexa 53
Making Alexa read to you 54
Learn to acquire Audiobooks for Alexa...................................54
Troubleshooting your gadget's Show Mode Charging Station
....54

CHAPTER 10 57
Parental Control..57
    Basic parental controls setup...57
    Utilizing Amazon Kids+ to set parental controls 58
    Manage your kid's or teen's profile 59
    How to decide when your child may use their tablet and establish a curfew 61
    Monitor or keep an eye on your kid's tablet use 62
    Using Amazon FreeTime Unlimited to purchase parental controls 62

    Subscribing to Amazon FreeTime Unlimited on an Amazon Fire 62

    Using Amazon FreeTime Unlimited's parental controls 63

    Disable Parental Controls on your Fire max 64

CHAPTER 11 65

Screen or display time 65

    Setting bedtime up on your gadget 65

        Create goals 66

        Using Smart Filters 66

    Manage your children's screen time on their fire max gadget 66

    Setting up a kid's account on a Fire Max 11 67

    Switch from your profile to your child's profile 69

    Limiting or restricting the amount of time used on your Fire gadget 70

Chapter 12 72

Managing content 72

    Set language preference 72

        To set language preferences, ... 72

        Share the books you've bought with your kid's profile. 72

        Install your children preferred videos to view when there's the absence of internet service 73

        Deleting paid stuff from your kid's profile 73

    Moving files to your Fire Max gadget 73

    Erasing or deleting files or content from your Fire max 74

CHAPTER 13 75

Learn to use the web browser on your fire max 11 75

Amazon Kids web browser...75
Open/Access Browser..75
    Bookmarks 76
Reading List...77
Silk Browser Left Menu..77
Reading View and Sharing 78
Switching profile 79
    Signing in or Authenticating during app startup.............79
    Utilizing the lock screen to log in....................................79
    Switching from Amazon Kids 79
    Creating passwords...79

CHAPTER 14 81

Create a Fingerprint, PIN, or Password, or use your Fire Max 11 to sign in. 81

    Using your Fire Max gadget to modify the Pin code or passcode for the lock screen 81

    Unlock your Amazon Fire 11 max 82

CHAPTER 15 83

Setting ups on your fire tablet 11 83

    Modify the Fire Tablet's Screen Brightness 83

    Change the Fire Tablet's screen's timeout setting.................83

    Adjusting the volume control on your fire max 84

    Mirror your Screen on Your Fire Max 11 84

    Setting Your Fire Tablet's Time or Clock 85

    Pairing your Fire tablet with a PC 85

        Pair your Amazon gadget with a cable. 86

Guide to Troubleshooting fire max 11 won't connect to other devices 90

CHAPTER 16 91

The camera on fire max 91

Usage guide for the camera on Fire max 91

Fixing your Tablet's Camera 91

CHAPTER 17 93

Troubleshooting your fire max 11 93

The Fire tablet won't charge 93

Tablet freezing 93

Wi-Fi won't work on the Fire 94

Significant battery drain 94

E or Digital-books disappearing or not functioning properly. 96

Micro SD card not functioning or not being recognized 97

Troubleshoot your Fire Max 11's fingerprint access. 98

Installing Google Play Store on your Fire Max 99

Advanced Options 101

Rooting a Fire Max 102

FIRE MAX 11 fEATURES

	Features	
1	O S	Fire OS
4	Display Size	Eleven inches
5	Screen Resolution	2,000 by 1,200 pixels
6	CPU	Mediatek MTK8188J
7	Storage Capacity	64 GB
8	Stylus pen	yes
9	Battery Life	Up to 14 hours
10	Keyboard	yes

INTRODUCTION

The Fire Max 11 ($229; available now) has a huge, clear screen, more horsepower beneath the hood, improved front and rear cameras, and two remarkable attachments. So, should you choose Amazon's newest tablets if you're looking for a device that will serve both your entertainment and productivity needs?

You are in for one of the greatest tablets in the tech sector so far with its bright, sleek design, expandable storage, optional keyboard cover, and pen.

One major benefit of the Fire Max 11 is expandable storage.

Both the front and back 8-megapixel cameras on the Fire Max 11 are more than enough for uses like zoom calls and simple photography.

If you're right-handed and using the tablet in landscape mode, the power and volume buttons are placed on the right edge, which makes sense because everything fits naturally beneath your right finger. The tablet may be unlocked just by placing your finger on the power button, which has fingerprint-ID capabilities.

The new Fire 11 stylus pen

This plastic pen works well for taking notes and drawing.

- The function button, which is not programmable
- Even though it automatically couples with the tablet,
- The Fire Max 11 allows you to take notes, sketch, and draw.

CHAPTER 1

Getting started

1. Turn on your tablet by pressing down the flank knob or button on your gadget

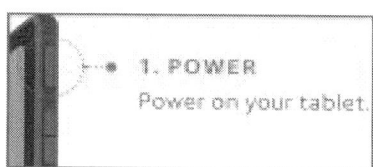

2. Swipe up to unlock
3. Follow the on-screen prompts to set up, join a wireless hotspot, enroll with an existing account, or register for a new one.

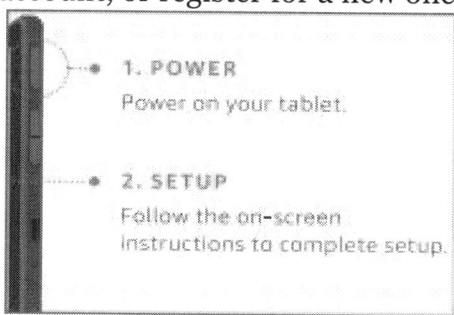

Putting a Sim card in a fire max 11 tablet

1. slot in the SIM card installation device or pin into the device's SIM card hole
2. Bring out the SIM card holder
3. Insert the SIM tray with the Nano-SIM card inside

4. Make sure the SIM card tray is properly placed and fastened by inserting it into the device.

Setting up your fire max gadget

Make sure you're close to an accessible Wi-Fi network because you'll need one to configure your Fire tablet. You must also have an Amazon account, although you can create one on your device if you don't already have one.

Depending on the generation of your Fire tablet, the options you see could change, but the procedure is essentially the same across all models.

1. Before turning it on, make sure your tablet is completely charged. and as you connect it in, pay attention to the battery indication. After charging your phone, hold down the Power button to switch it on.

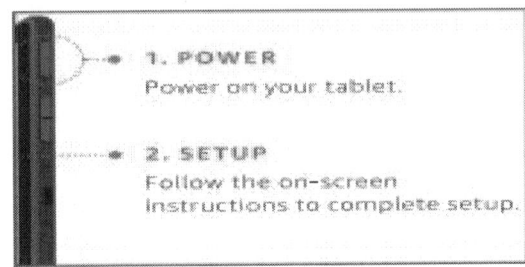

2. Select your preferred language and font size, then hit Continue

5

3. Input the passcode after choosing the Wi-Fi service you intend to pair/connect to. Any updates that your Fire tablet requires will be downloaded automatically.
4. To generate a new account, hit on Start here or input your Amazon login details.

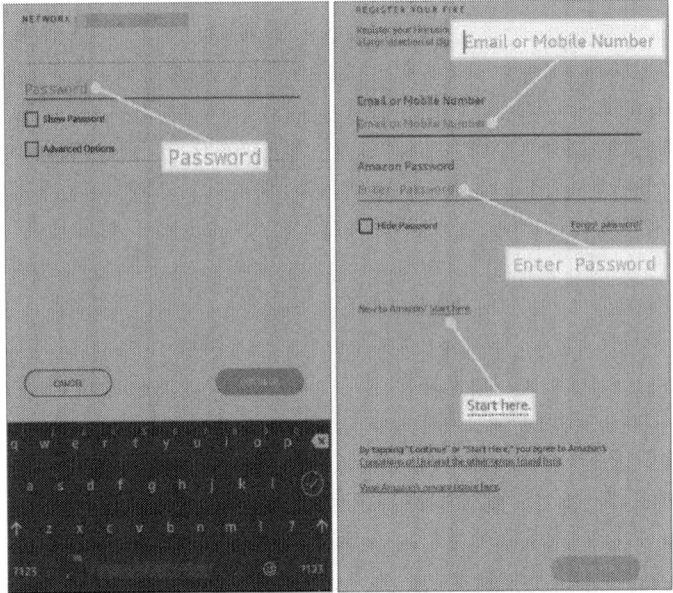

5. If your Amazon account has backed up the info via your prior gadgets, you will be able to hit on Restore to load all of its applications. To start with the default settings in any other case, hit Do Not Restore.
6. Look through the features, deselect any that you don't want, and then hit Continue.

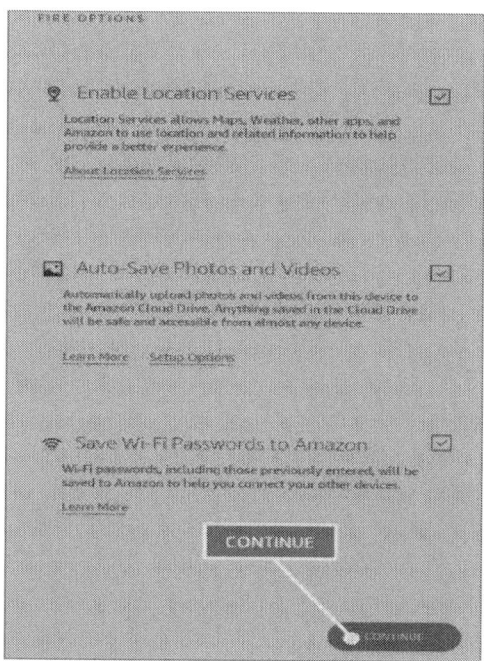

7. After watching a brief introduction video, choose the Amazon account profiles that will be utilizing the device. You will be required to enter a lock screen passcode or PIN if you add a kid profile.
8. You could receive promotions for Amazon services like Kindle Unlimited, Prime, and Goodreads. Accept the setup offer; you may always join up for these services later.
9. After that, Amazon will suggest media like games, applications, and movies. Choose the things you wish to download, or choose Not lNow to stop
10. The process of configuring the Alexa voice assistant will then be explained to you. Choose Disable Alexa, then hit Continue, or select Agree & Continue.

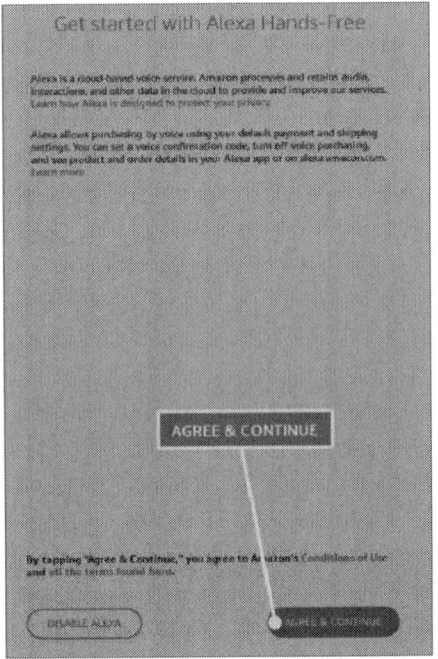

11. Hit on Finish to retrace yourself back to the home display of your Fire Max gadget. You are now prepared to use your smartphone after closing any pop-up windows.

Forgot to set up a password when setting Up My Fire Tablet?

Go to Settings > Security & Privacy > Lock Screen Passcode if you forgot to set up a password when you first installed your smartphone. You should also enable parental restrictions on your Fire tablet if your youngster intends to use it.

CHAPTER 2

Connecting your Fire Max 11 tablet to the Internet

Any Wi-Fi network may be used to connect the Fire tablet, giving you access to the internet and all of the tablet's features. You may join the Fire tab to any public network, even your personal home Wi-Fi network if you have the necessary login details.

Method 1: linking or pairing to an accessible Wi-Fi service

1. Slide downward via the upper section of the display screen on your Fire gadget & hit on **Wireless**

2. Make sure the Aeroplane Mode switch is set to "Off."

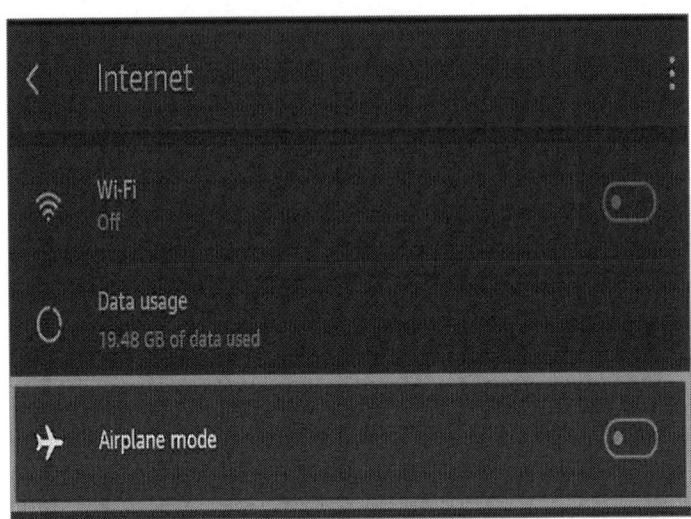

3. After selecting "Wi-Fi," select "On" next to Wi-Fi. The screen will provide a catalog of Wi-Fi services that are accessible.

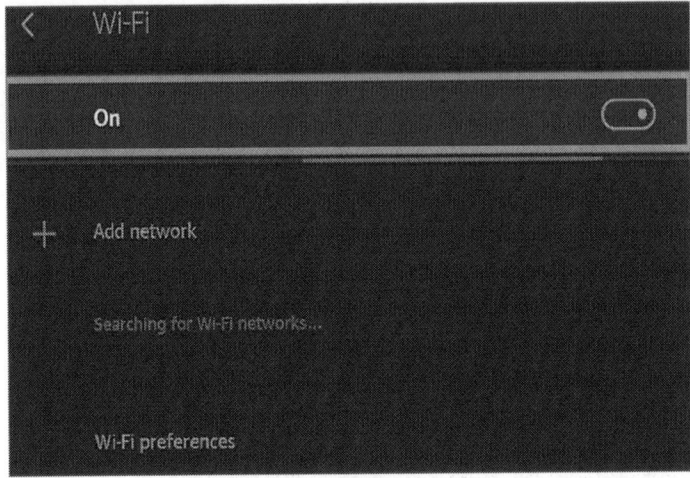

4. To connect, tap the wifi network you wish to use. You'll need to provide a pin code to utilize any networks marked with a lock symbol.
5. If prompted, enter the password before selecting **Connect**. Your Fire gadget will then pair to the Internet through that precise network.

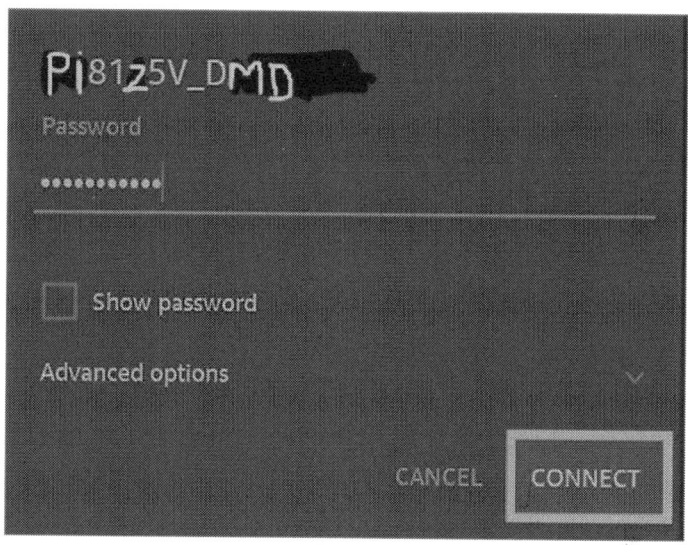

Manually Adding a Wi-Fi Network in Method 2

1. From the top of your screen, swipe down and select "Wireless."
2. Confirm that Aeroplane Mode is turned "Off."
3. Hit on Wi-Fi before toggling it to On
4. select "add or Join Other Network."

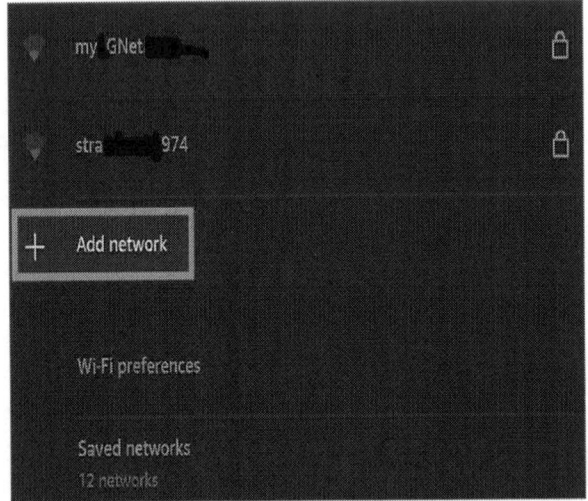

5. In the "Network SSID" text area, type the name of your network.
6. Choose a network security type from the dropdown menu next to "Security" by clicking on it.
7. If necessary, enter the network password before selecting "Save." Then, the Internet will be accessible on your Fire Max.

CHAPTER 3

Making Calls and receiving a call

1. First, press the Phone symbol in the app grid or carousel on the home screen to make a call or listen to your voicemail
2. Tap the Keypad icon to manually input a number
3. Type the desired telephone number and choose Call
4. Press the History icon, choose a call from the list, and then press it to return it
5. To call a contact, hit the Contacts icon, and then choose the person's name from the list
6. Use the phone number in the contact information by tapping it to make a call
7. Press the Keypad symbol, then press Call to show the last number you typed, to redial it.
8. Press Call
9. Hold down the Home button while saying "call" or "dial," then speak the name of a contact or recite a phone number.

Using a Fire tablet to make a video call

1. Launch the Alexa application on your smart gadget or Fire tablet
2. From the navigation bar at the bottom, choose Communicate

3. Via the upper section, hit on the Call knob or button
4. Select the individual you want to reach out to.
5. To place an audio or video call, choose or hit on their phone no or one of the Alexa knobs or buttons.

To begin a video call from a Fire tablet

1. Open the Alexa app,
2. Choose the Communicate tab,
3. Pick your contact, and press the video call icon
   - You may naturally end a video call by pressing the stop button on the display

Note: On a compatible mobile device, download the Alexa app before you start. To utilize Alexa Communication services like announcements or phoning, you also need a working mobile number.

- Switch on your gadget's Alexa application.
- Choosing Communicate.
- A contacts icon should be chosen.
- To access your communication settings, choose your name
- Pick the designation of your kid
- If there is an Amazon Kids profile, the child's name is displayed
- Choose Add New Contact
- Choose one or more contacts and add them to your child's list of authorized contacts.

CHAPTER 4

Texting and mailing messages on your Fire max 11

Configure Your Fire Tablet for Email

Utilize the details from your current email account to configure the Email app on your tablet.

1. From the Home screen, choose the Email app
2. After inputting your mail info, hit on Next.
3. Select Next after entering your current email account's password
4. Select Go to Inbox after setting up your email account.

Receiving Emails on your Fire Max 11 gadget

You must configure the Fire's built-in email software if you wish to receive emails on the device. Here is the procedure, which is quite easy to follow:

1. From the home screen of your Fire, launch the Email app. If the app isn't there, click on Apps at the top of the screen and you should be able to locate it there.
2. If you are opening the app for the first time, it will prompt you to input the email address you

wish to use with it. Click the text field next to your email address
3. Fill out the box with the email you wish to use with the app
4. Press Next
5. Type in the email account's password
6. Click Next
7. Tap the Add Another Account option and repeat steps 1-6 if you wish to add other accounts for your tablet to receive emails from.

Messages that have been sent to the addresses you have connected to the app should now download, and you may access them in the Inbox portion of the app.

Getting SMS and MMS Messages on a Fire 11 gadget

You'll need to download a third-party app from the Amazon App Store to be able to send and receive text and multimedia messages on your Fire tablet. TextMe, a premium service that allows users to send and receive free text messages in the US and Canada, is one of the better and most user-friendly solutions.

You may even create several different phone numbers so that your relatives and friends who live abroad can still get in touch with you. Additionally, you may make and receive phone calls using these numbers, giving your gadget some much-needed functionality

You must perform the following actions to set up a number where others may message you:

1. From the home screen of your Fire, launch the TextMe app

2. Hit on the Me icon at the downward right angle of the display screen
3. Click "My Numbers"
4. Press the Get new phone number button
5. To add to your device, decide whether to add a local or an international number.

Send your number to the individuals you want to be able to message you after it has been set up or use the app to send them a message, and they will be able to SMS and MMS you.

CHAPTER 5

How to Use an Amazon Fire Tablet as a New or Experienced User

You must follow a few steps to establish an account and protect your device if this is your first time using an Amazon Fire tablet or if you recently bought one but haven't yet set it up.

1. The Amazon Fire tablet's button controls are straightforward. The tablet's power button, volume controls, and micro-USB charging connection are located on its top
2. If you have the most recent Amazon Fire 10 tablet, it has a 5-megapixel camera with no flash on the back.
3. You must set up your first login PIN when you initially charge and turn on your Amazon Fire tablet. The tablet will utilize this each time it is turned on. Anything with four digits can be this.
4. For any account you intend to use with this tablet or gadget, you will be asked to input your sign-up details as one of the starting processes.Log in using your usual Amazon account email and password for the quickest access to all of your Amazon items and services.

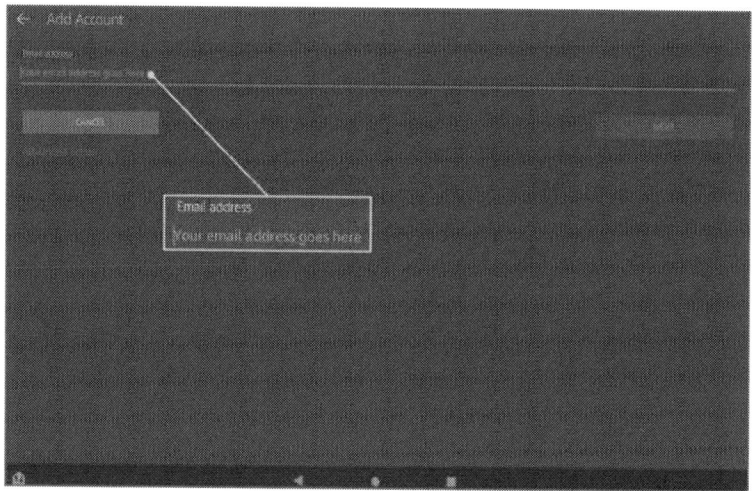

5. To add additional family members to your gadget, open the Settings app and go to Profiles & Family Library. This includes kid-specific accounts with parental restrictions and restricted access. Additionally, you may here set up parental controls for every one of those child accounts.

Instructions for Using & Navigating the Fire Interface

Although it differs differently from other tablets you may have used in the past, using the Amazon Fire tablet is straightforward.

1. After logging in, a home screen with three menu choices will be displayed. On your Amazon Fire tablet, all of the installed apps may be found under the Home menu, which is the default.

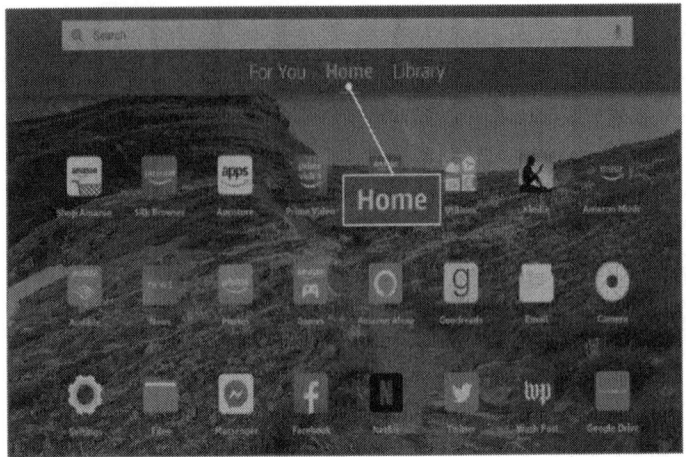

2. Like other tablets, this one includes Quick Settings icons on the screen that, when swiping down from the top, let you enable or disable certain tablet features. These include display mode, Bluetooth hands-free, wireless, airplane mode, blue shade (night mode), do not disturb, auto-rotate, and Alexa hands-free.
3. The Amazon Fire tablet makes it incredibly easy to move between numerous open apps. Simply swipe left or right across the tablet screen to navigate. This will make your open applications appear in a sliding display. When you locate the open app you want to utilize, just stop swiping and press it to return to full screen.
4. By selecting the Library option on the home screen, you may access items from your various Amazon content libraries, including Audible audiobooks, Amazon Prime videos, and content from any other Amazon services to which you have enrolled.

5. You may customize the majority of the tablet's functionality by going to the Settings app. For instance, you may add Bluetooth devices or link up to Wi-Fi networks and the Internet. You may change Alexa settings, sound or device settings, and more.

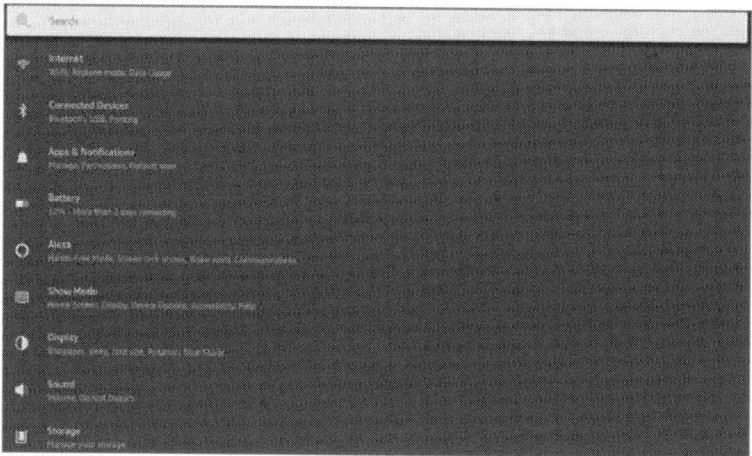

6. You may use your tablet to connect to smart devices via the Devices app on Amazon Fire. Once you've connected smart devices, you can

use the applications to operate those apps or give Alexa voice commands because the digital assistant is built right into the Amazon Fire tablet.

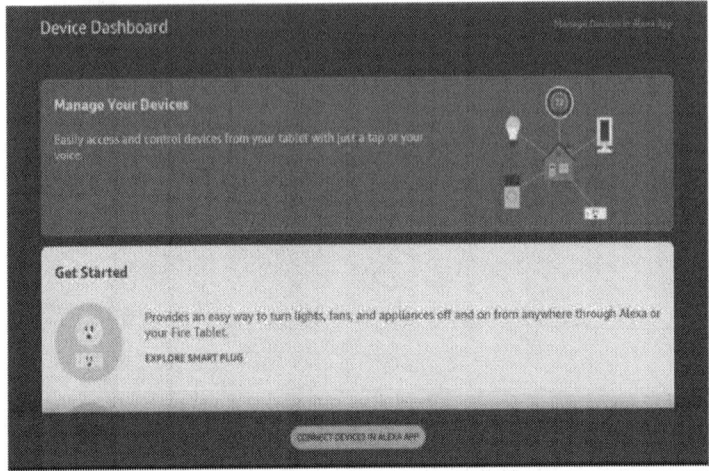

Adding Applications to your fire max tablet

You can surf the internet, watch and listen to media, and do a lot more using the apps and services that come preloaded on the Amazon Fire tablet. However, the Amazon Appstore app makes it simple to install new programs.

1. Another thing you might have noticed is that You'll see a selection of Amazon apps in place of Google or Apple apps on this tablet

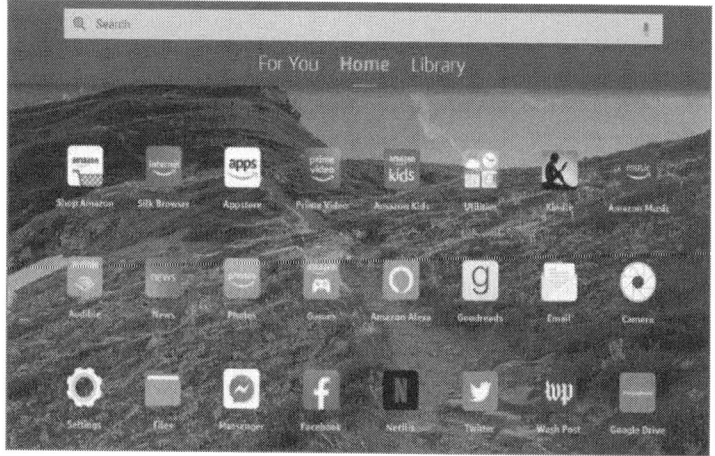

2. There are several pre-installed features on the Amazon Fire tablet, including a clock, calendar, calculator, and even maps.

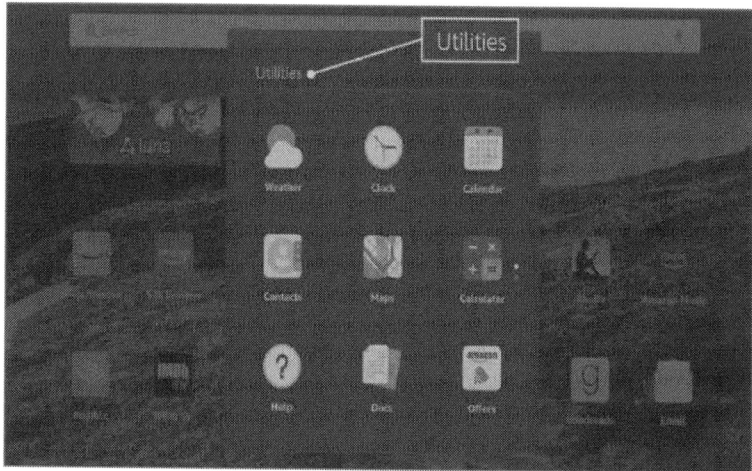

3. You will be able to increase the number of applications on your Amazon Fire tablet by utilizing the Amazon Appstore app. By choosing the Categories option, you will be able to install programs in several different categories. The highlighted applications are

listed under the Home page, while the Videos tab concentrates on Amazon video content, the Family tab contains kid-friendly apps, Best Sellers shows the most downloaded apps and the For You tab lists apps that are relevant to the apps you already have installed.

4. To install an app, simply tap it and choose the GET option.

Utilizing the new fire max Web Browser

The Amazon Fire tablet comes with the Silk browser already installed.

1. To open the Silk browser, first tap on the Home screen.

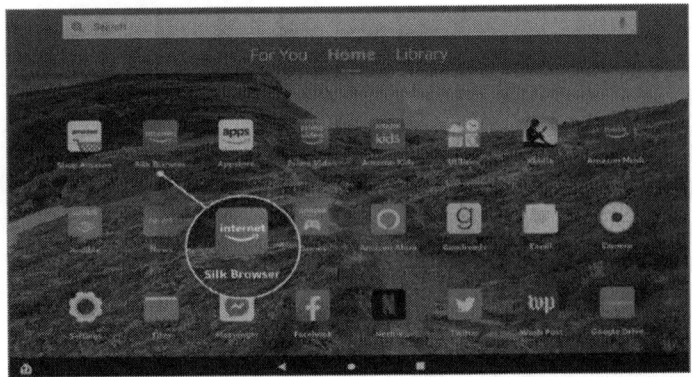

2. Silk is a rather basic browser, but the three dots menu in the top right has a variety of integrated capabilities. These include opening bookmarks, browsing prior history or downloads, accessing your Amazon reading or buying lists, choosing the Dark theme, or

opening a "Private tab" (this is comparable to Google's Incognito mode).

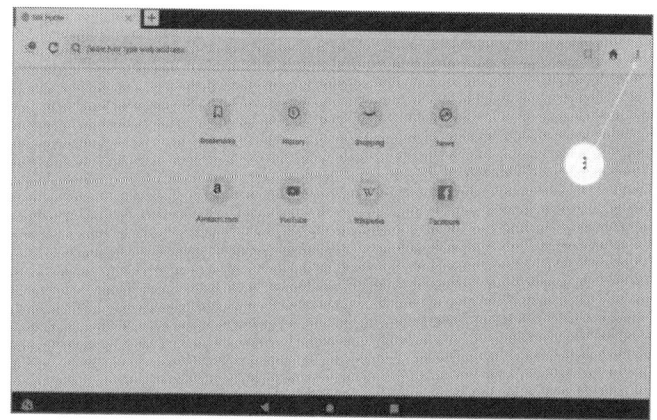

3. Click Settings to modify the browser's settings.

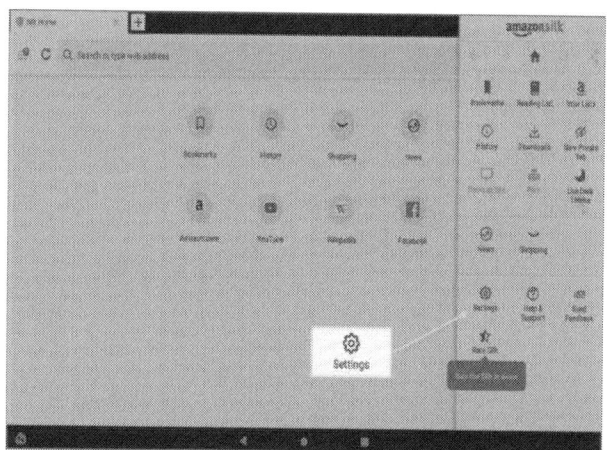

4. Settings choices include changing the default search engine, modifying browser security settings, storing passwords, and preserving payment information.

← Silk Settings

Payment methods

Passwords

Addresses and more

Accessibility

Silk Home

Privacy and security

Advanced settings

CHAPTER 6

Rebooting the iPad

Restart your tablet to resolve everything.

1. Tap the Power Off option while continuing to depress the power button.
2. If you keep holding down the power button, your device (iPad) will turn back on.
3. Open the Play Store from the home screen once it has started up and check to see whether everything functions as it should.
4. When you're setting up the Play Store, it's simple to overlook this step, but doing so can help you fix your device quickly.

Delete or clean out all app data.

1. Launch the Settings program.
2. Hit on and Choose the Apps & Notifications section (or any other part with the words "Apps" or "Applications" in it).
3. Tap Manage All Applications
4. In the list of apps, look for the Play Store and choose it.
5. To stop the Play Store from operating, tap the Force Stop button.
6. Select the Clear Data (also known as Clear storage) menu item under the Storage menu option.
7. Check to check if your app functions as intended by going back to the Play Store app.

If it still didn't work, repeat the procedure above but this time restart your tablet before accessing the Play Store. Attempting to stop and clear the caches of the Play Store and Google Play Services should be your next step if the first method didn't work.

CHAPTER 7

Storage and SD cards

Inserting and removing sd card

Instructions for Adding an SD Card to a Fire Tablet

The ease and convenience of installing an SD card is one of the finest features of the Fire tablet. You'll learn later how to utilize the card as a mass-storage device or for internal storage. Installing it is simple. The process is as follows.

Here are the actions to take:

1. Press and hold the "Power/Sleep" button for two seconds while selecting "Power off" to switch off your tablet.
2. Find your tablet's SD card slot.

3. Use the pointed instrument to pry open the door enclosing the card slot. To achieve this, you can use a flat-bladed screwdriver, a knife,

or your fingernail. It's vital to understand that the door covering doesn't entirely separate from your device. Instead, it makes a downward pivot

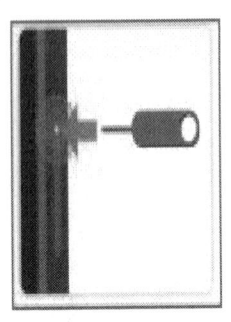

4. When you hear a clicking sound, gently push down on each side of the card and put it into the socket.

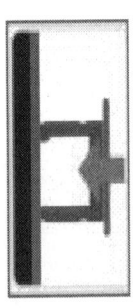

5. Gently reposition the gadget's door covering to its closed position. This will stop dust from collecting in the slot

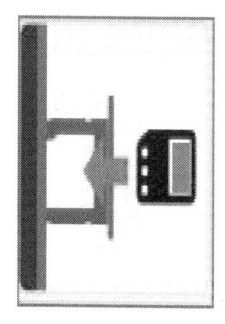

Once you've completed these procedures, your device ought to recognize the SD card and signal

How to Store Data on an SD Card Using a Fire Tablet

The SD card format is not recognized by the system when you attach it to your tablet; it is identified as an "unsupported storage device." Your smartphone ought to be ready for usage after only a couple of extra steps.

Two choices should appear if you hit the "unsupported storage device" notification:

1. Utilize as more storage for the tab or your new gadget
2. Apply as a portable storage

Using an SD Card with a Fire Tablet for Portable Storage

Here's how to do it if you simply want to utilize your card to store media files:

1. When your tablet recognizes the card, select "PORTABLE STORAGE."

2. Your tablet will now prompt you to decide whether to format the device. Trail the guidelines on the screen of the gadget to accomplish this. If the card has any files you intend to save, you can skip this phase.

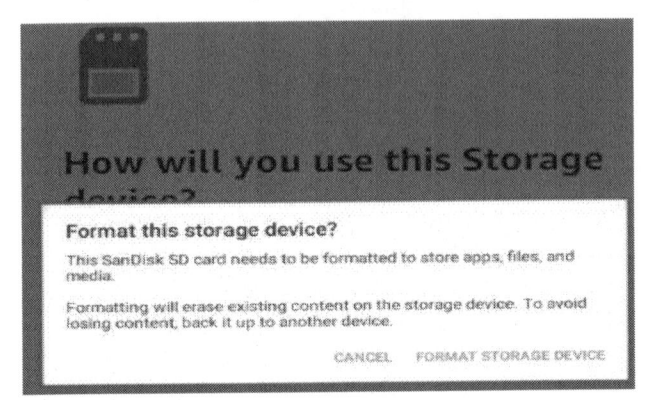

   Format this storage device?
   This SanDisk SD card needs to be formatted to store apps, files, and media.
   Formatting will erase existing content on the storage device. To avoid losing content, back it up to another device.
   CANCEL   FORMAT STORAGE DEVICE

3. Go to the settings on your tablet and select Storage

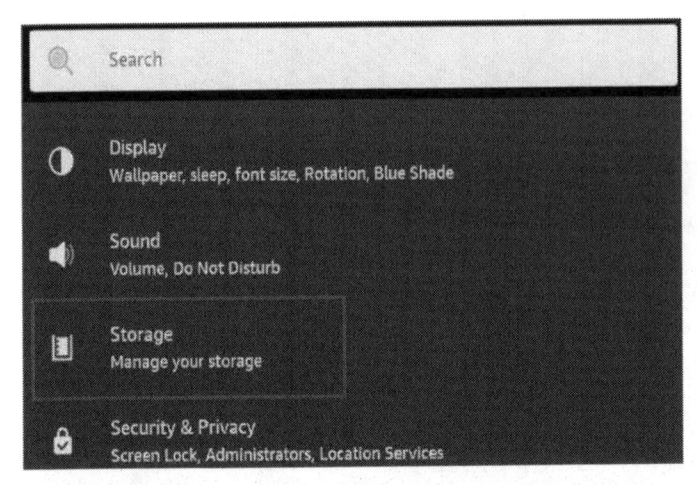

   Display
   Wallpaper, sleep, font size, Rotation, Blue Shade

   Sound
   Volume, Do Not Disturb

   Storage
   Manage your storage

   Security & Privacy
   Screen Lock, Administrators, Location Services

4. Click "Internal Storage" to display a list of your device's installed apps, sorted by the ones that have consumed the most space.

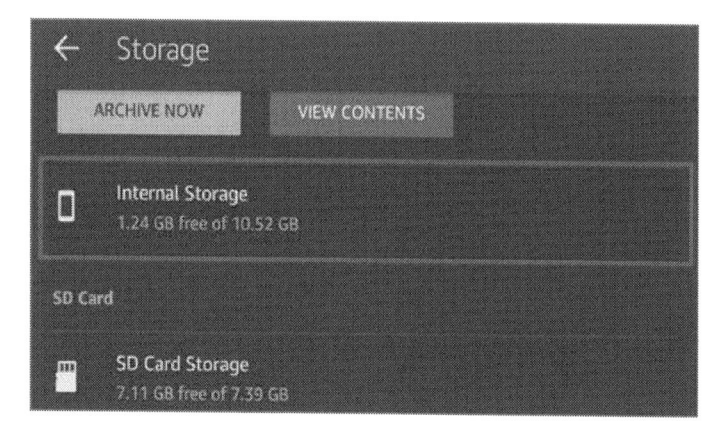

[screenshot: Storage screen showing Archive Now, View Contents, Internal Storage 1.24 GB free of 10.52 GB, SD Card Storage 7.11 GB free of 7.39 GB]

5. Continue to the bottom until you see "SD Card Storage." Below this, you ought to find several toggle switches that allow you to pick which objects to download to the card. These choices include the following:

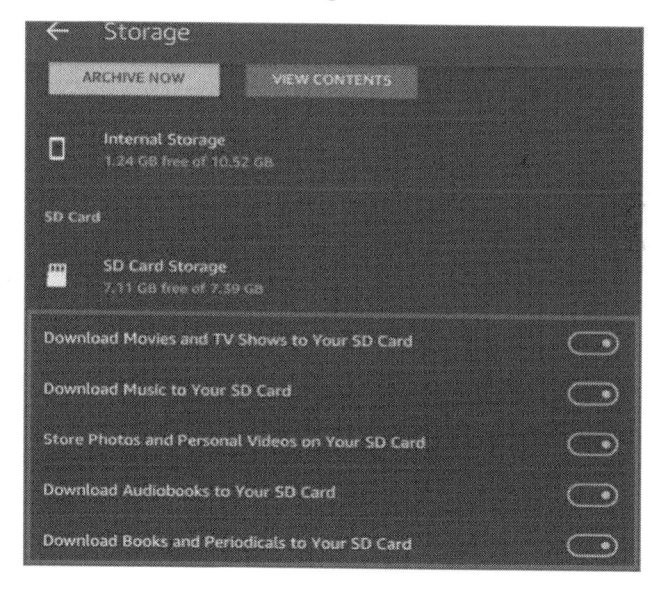

[screenshot: Storage screen with toggles for Download Movies and TV Shows to Your SD Card, Download Music to Your SD Card, Store Photos and Personal Videos on Your SD Card, Download Audiobooks to Your SD Card, Download Books and Periodicals to Your SD Card]

- Movies and TV shows may be downloaded to your SD Card

- Download music on your SD card and save it there along with your videos and photos.
- Audiobooks may be downloaded to SD cards.
- Save periodicals and books to your memory card.

All of the aforementioned settings will be turned on by default. Put the switch next to it in the "off" position if you don't want to use your card for any of the choices provided.

Any downloaded files will then be saved on the card. Keep in mind that if you remove the card, you'll immediately lose access to whatever is stored on it.

Utilizing SD Cards as Internal Storage and formatting your card

The following actions must be taken if you wish to use the card to host programs or store files:

1. When your tablet recognizes the card, select "Use for extra tablet storage." If the card is already being utilized for portable storage in any other case:
   - Activate Settings
   - Choose Storage
   - Format as Internal Storage which is located under SD Card Storage.
2. To format your card, adhere to the on-screen instructions.

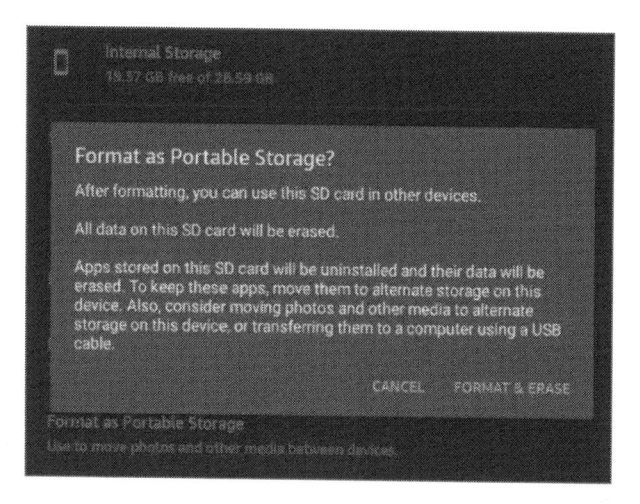

> **Format as Portable Storage?**
>
> After formatting, you can use this SD card in other devices.
>
> All data on this SD card will be erased.
>
> Apps stored on this SD card will be uninstalled and their data will be erased. To keep these apps, move them to alternate storage on this device. Also, consider moving photos and other media to alternate storage on this device, or transferring them to a computer using a USB cable.
>
> CANCEL FORMAT & ERASE

3. After formatting the card, your tablet will prompt you to choose whether you want to "move content" to the card right immediately or "move later."

> **Move content to storage device?**
>
> You can now move files, media and certain apps to this SanDisk SD card. This will take about 4 minutes, and will free 2.66 GB of internal device storage.
>
> During the move:
> - Don't remove the Storage device.
> - Keep your device charged.
> - Some apps won't work.
>
> MOVE CONTENT LATER   MOVE CONTENT

If you select "move content," all media assets, including music, movies, and videos, will be instantly transferred to your card. No applications will be transferred, though.

If you select "move content later," you may move files whenever you wish with the extra benefit of being able to move both files and programs.

Utilize these procedures to transfer applications to your SD card:

1. Go to the settings on your tablet and select Storage

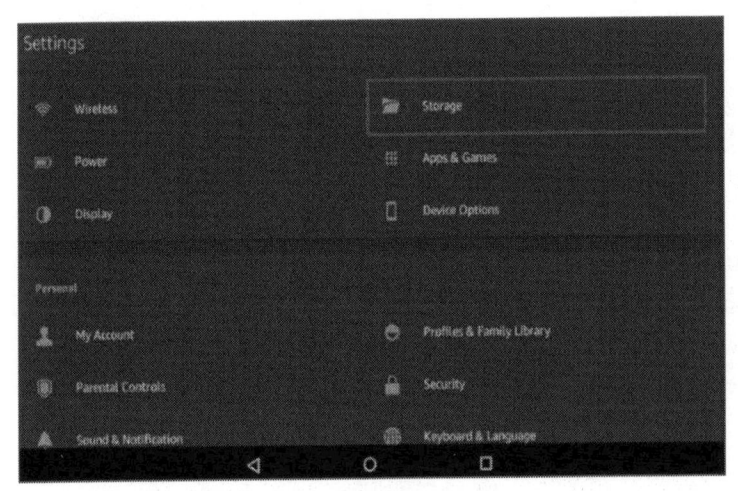

2. choose "Internal Storage"
3. Select Move Apps to SD Card" under "SD Card

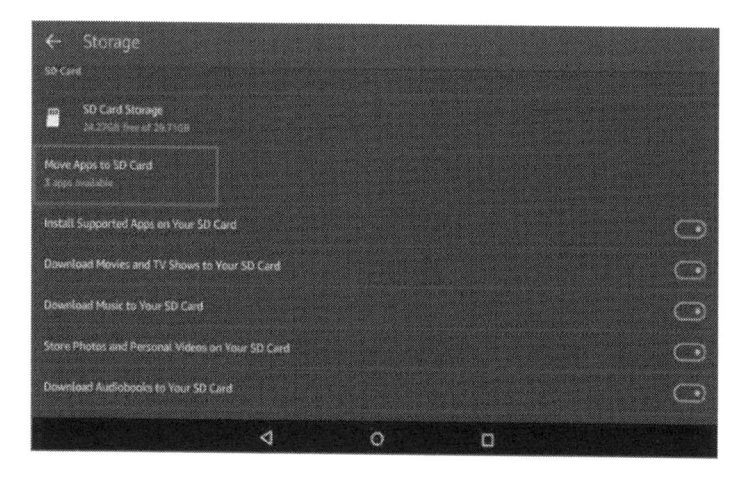

Your Fire OS will now assess the apps that can be transferred directly to your card. Apps that cannot fit on your card will still be stored on your tablet's internal storage, though.

Expanding your storage space

With Amazon's most current tablet, expandable storage is thankfully still an option, making it simple and inexpensive to add hundreds of extra gigabytes of storage. We've chosen some of our finest microSD cards for Fire Tablets, with capacities of up to 1TB. Drop it into the proper location on your tablet after choosing the size that best suits your requirements.

Format your storage

1. Put the microSD card in your tablet's card slot.
2. A pop-up window inquiring how you plan to utilize the SD card fills the screen. Choose "Use as internal storage"
3. If prompted, choose Format storage device to allow formatting of the card.
4. Allow the format to go on.
5. Once it's done, go to the Storage section of the settings to see how much space is on your SD card and choose which material to automatically transfer to your external storage. Individually turn on your preferred options.
6. Choose Format as Internal Storage from this screen, then choose Format & Erase from the popup that appears if you wish to utilize it for apps and games. This action is optional. If you'd rather utilize your SD card for music or movies, you may leave it as is.

Your SD card can be deleted or removed using this settings option.

CHAPTER 8

Wireless Keyboard, Detachable Case with stylus pen

Install your device

1. To secure it in place, gently hit on the lower section of your gadget into the case
2. Next, insert the upper half of your gadget into the case. Examine each corner to ensure it is firmly secured.

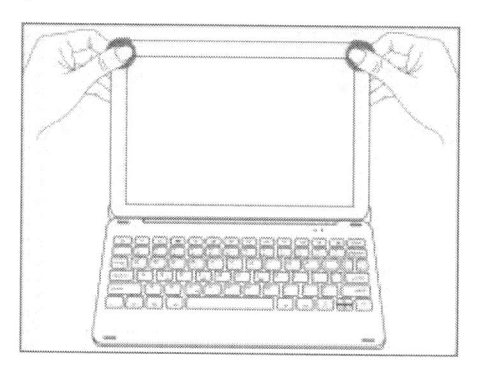

Remove your device

1. Gently pull the rear cover off the tablet while holding it on both sides with your thumbs.
2. Proceed GENTLY to peel the cover
3. Take tablet out

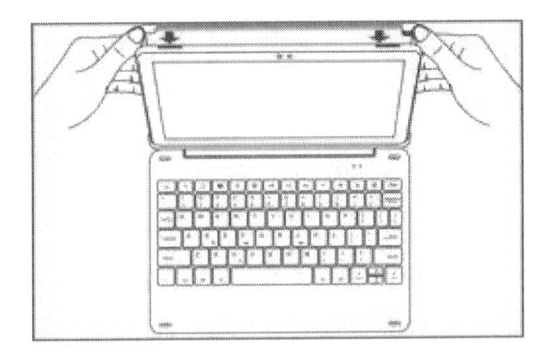

Detaching your gadget's keyboard

The keyboard and rear cover are made to be separated from one another. They magnetically link to one another.

Pairing Solution

1. Toggle On/Off to toggle your keyboard On
2. Hit on the Fn + C knobs together to go into pairing mode
3. Authenticate your gadget's Bluetooth setup are on
4. Select Settings - Bluetooth – On
5. Select "Pair new device".
6. To finish pairing, choose **Fintie Keyboard** via the list of suitable gadgets on your device.
7. Choose "Fintie Keyboard"; after linking, the Bluetooth pairing indication will disappear

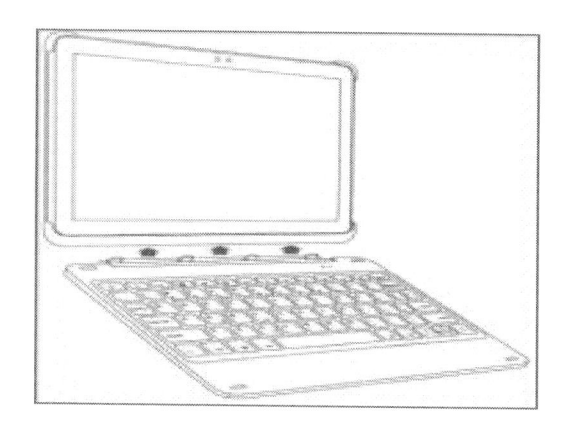

Put the keyboard in Sleep Mode

After 30 min of inactivity, the keyboard goes into sleep mode. To make it work,

- After pressing any key, pause for 3 secs.

Charging your keyboard

1. Attach one USB end of the charging cable to your preferred USB charger, and the other Type-C end to the keyboard.
2. When it is charging, the power meter will become red. Usually, it takes 4 hours to charge completely. (Output: 500mA at 5V DC.)

Synchronizing a Bluetooth keyboard with your device

When you have both of them, you can combine them.

1. Slide down the top menu after turning on and unlocking your Amazon Fire.
2. To access your wifi settings, tap "Wireless": (You can also select "More+" and then "Wireless," but that's an extra step you don't need to do.)

3. Tap "Bluetooth" and then "On" to turn it on.

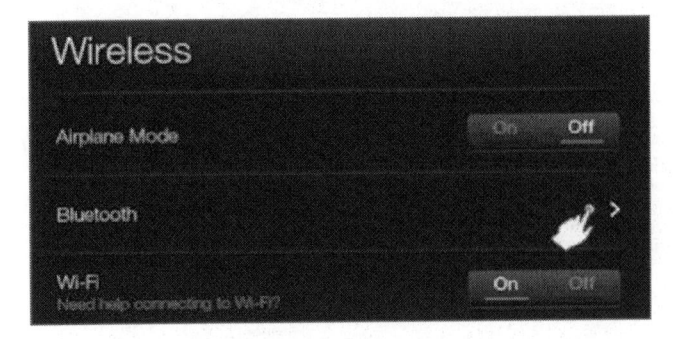

4. Now switch on your Bluetooth keyboard for the Fire device and press the connect button (located on the back of the device). Please be aware that the batteries must be installed first for it to operate

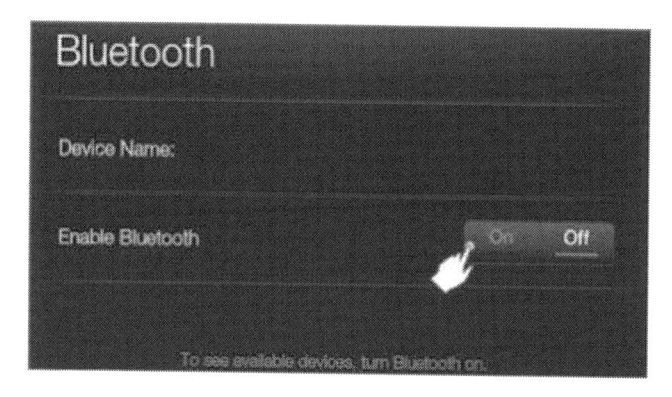

5. Hit on the "Search for devices" switch at the lower section of your gadget.

6. The "AmazonBasics Keyboard" ought to be shown among the available devices when you next view a list of them. Click this

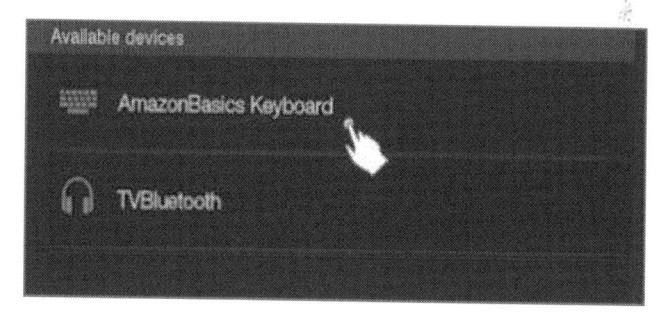

7. The keyboard should begin "pairing," a jargon-filled word that just indicates that it is connecting

> Available devices
>
> AmazonBasics Keyboard
> Pairing...

8. There will be a pairing demand

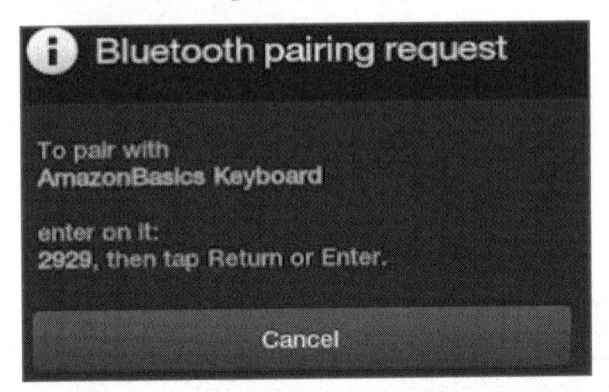

> **Bluetooth pairing request**
>
> To pair with
> AmazonBasics Keyboard
>
> enter on it:
> 2929, then tap Return or Enter.
>
> Cancel

9. As instructed, enter the four-digit number that appears on YOUR screen, not the one shown in the image above, and then press the Enter/Return key.

Your Bluetooth keyboard and Fire Max should now be linked after a little delay:

CHAPTER 9

Using Alexa on your new Fire Tablet

With its useful features, Amazon's voice-activated personal assistant Alexa has become indispensable to many people. Your dependable helper can accompany you everywhere you go if your Fire tablet has Alexa support.

Learn how to call Alexa from a distance and by touch on your Fire tablet.

How to Make Alexa Work (activate) on Your Fire Tablet

To make Alexa available on your Fire tablet:

1. Sliding right from your Home screen will take you to the Apps tab, where you may search for Alexa.
2. Get the mobile Alexa app.
3. After installation, tap Amazon Alexa on your Home screen to launch it.

4. Give your name, then choose Continue
5. Enter your phone number to set up phone verification, then validate the code that is delivered to you.

You may begin utilizing Amazon's voice assistant after a quick instruction.

Utilizing Alexa with your Fire tablet

1. If you wish to control Alexa with your voice, hold down the Home icon (the circle in the bottom center of your screen) and watch for a blue line to appear. Then, you may issue a directive or pose a query

2. You may access the settings menu by tapping the hamburger menu in the top-left corner of the Alexa app's home screen. To understand how Alexa can assist, hit Things to Try, then tap a topic. To locate new Alexa skills, just say, "Alexa, suggest new skills," or click on Skills & Games.

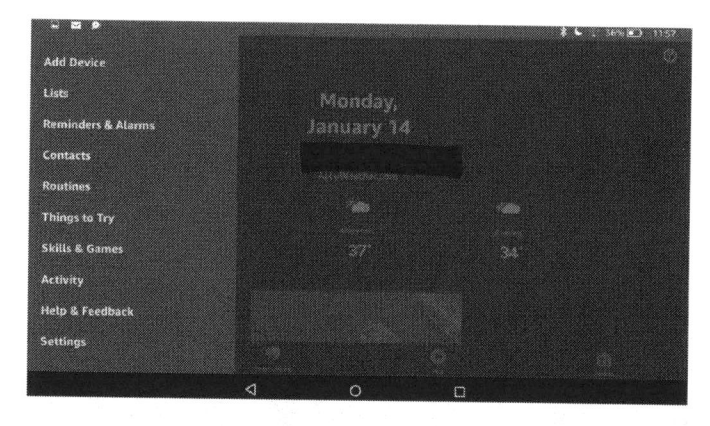

Installing Alexa on your new fire max gadget

If the Alexa application is not already installed on your Fire Max tab, you may manually download it via the following

1. Swipe right on your Home screen until you reach the "Apps" page.
2. Type in "Alexa" in the search bar.
3. Download the "Amazon Alexa" app.

Steps to set Alexa up on your Fire tablet

1. Select the "Amazon Alexa" application via your Home display screen.
2. Click Continue once you've inputted your designation.
3. Input your gadgets number if you want to enable your gadget verification.
4. To begin utilising the voice assistant, adhere to a quick training.

Utilizing Touch to call Alexa on your new Fire Tab

Follow these steps to touch-call Alexa:

To call Alexa with a touch, trail these steps:

1. Long-press the "Home" button after swiping up from the bottom of your screen to see the navigation bar.

2. Ask Alexa something once you see a brilliant blue line.

If nothing happens when you hit on & hold the Home knob or button on your Fire Max gadget, Alexa is not active. In that case, do the following to fix it:

1. via the tablet's upper section, slide downward
2. Hit on the "Settings" icon
1. Hit on "Device Options" via the tab.
2. Slide the switch next to "Alexa" to on

There may occasionally be no Alexa switch available in the Device Options. If it's absent from your gadget, you ought to upgrade your operating system. Check out how to update the Fire tablet as follows:

1. Via the upper of your tablet's display screen, slide downward.
2. Launch **Settings**
3. Hit on **Device Options**
4. Move below to the **System Updates** page.
5. Click the **Check now** menu knob. Trail the instructions provided on the screen to finish the process.

After upgrading your system, turn on the toggle for Alexa and try pressing the Home button while holding it down to ask Alexa a question. Try turning off parental controls if there is still no blue line.

Use your Fire tablet's Alexa hands-free mode

Remotely control smart home appliances using your new gadget

1. Slide downward via the upper section of the home display & hit on the Alexa Hands-Free icon to activate or deactivate Alexa hands-free.
2. Certain Alexa capabilities need you to input the PIN or password if you've set one up on your device. If you want to prevent Alexa from speaking to you when the device is locked:

   - From the Home screen of your tablet, swipe down and choose Settings.
   - Choose Alexa.
   - Choose Hands-Free Lock Screen Access in step 3.

Setting fire max 11 Show Mode Charging Dock up

Setting your Show Mode Charging Dock up involves:

1. Verifying that the software on your Fire tablet is up to date. Slide downward via the upper of the screen & click the Settings (gear) icon. Then select System Update from the Device Options menu. Install any pending software updates by selecting Check for Updates.
2. Slightly extend the USB connector tab on the tablet casing. After that, mount the shell onto your tablet and join the micro USB cable to the device's power port.

3. Connect the power cord and adapter that are provided to the adjustable stand.
4. Dock your tablet so that the magnetic charging connections are in contact with the stand.

To take your Fire tablet out of the case:

- Take your Fire tablet out of the charging dock for show mode
- Before taking off the tablet's shell, manually disconnect the USB connection tab from the charging port
- Take the Fire tablet's shell off.

Utilize the Show Mode Charging Dock

When you put your gadget in the Show Mode Charging Dock, it immediately enters Show Mode if you've set Automatic Mode Switching.

You will be able to activate Automatic Mode Switching by:

1. On the Home screen, slide downward via the peak of the screen, and then click the Settings (gear) logo
2. In the options menu, select Show Mode
3. Switch Automatic Mode Switching to "on."

Toggle your fire max gadget to show the mode

Using your tablet as a visual display, you may interact with Alexa from a distance.

Activate show mode on your gadget

- Slide downward via the upper section of your gadget's home display screen & hit on the Show Mode toggle or switch to toggle the mode on. The alternate command is to voice out the word "Alexa" and change to Show Mode."

Turn off or disable show mode on your device

- You may disable Show Mode by swiping down from the top of the screen, turning the Show Mode switch to "off," or asking Alexa to do so.

Read Kindle Books via Alexa

If you don't have an Audible account, Alexa can still read your books aloud. Simply say "Alexa, play the Kindle book" followed by the title to have Alexa read to you in her computerized voice.

After that, you may tell Alexa to pause, continue, or end your Kindle book. You may use more commands like these as well:

- Alexa, make the reading louder
- Tell Alexa to end reading after 30 minutes.
- Alexa what is the subsequent chapter

Making Alexa read to you

On a Fire tablet, tap anywhere on the display to see the available apps. Then, hit the Play icon in the bottom-right corner to activate Alexa's narration.

Learn to acquire Audiobooks for Alexa

Individual audiobooks can be bought at Amazon.com, the Audible app, or the Audible website. As an alternative, you may do the following to add Audible narration to ebooks you've previously bought from Amazon:

1. Go to Amazon.com & select Account & Lists from the top navigation menu.
2. Choose Your content and devices
3. Choose to Manage Digital Content
4. Next to the book you wish to add narration to, select the ellipses (...)
5. Make the option to Add Narration via the menu that shows.

Troubleshooting your gadget's Show Mode Charging Station

1. Problem: When the tablet is placed on the Show Mode Charging Dock, nothing happens.
    - Be certain your Fire tablet's software is up to date. Hit on the Settings (gear) logo & glide your thumb downward via the upper portion of the screen. Then select System Update from the Device Options menu. By choosing Check for

Updates, download all awaiting software updates.
- Ensure that the gadget has Alexa enabled. When placed on the dock without Alexa turned on, the gadget charges but does not go into Show Mode.
- Ensure that the micro USB connection is inserted into the charging port and that the Fire tablet is firmly clipped into the tablet case
- Verify the dock's power cord. The adapter must be linked to an operational outlet, and the cable must be securely hooked into the rear of the dock and the adapter
- Ensure that the tablet's magnetic connections are attached to the dock. There are two tiny metal contacts on the gadget shell's rear. Two metal pins on the dock are magnetically connected to the contacts. The gadget does not charge or go into Show Mode unless these connections are in contact
- By entering the Settings menu, choosing Show Mode, and turning the Automatic Mode Switching setting to "on," you can make sure that it is active.

2. Problem: The device takes longer to charge while utilizing the Show Mode Charging Dock.
   - If you often use your Fire tablet when it is docked, then this could be expected.

- To reduce charging time, put the gadget in standby mode. For the screen to be turned off, press the power button.

CHAPTER 10

Parental Control

Children may use the new tab to access social media, play games, view films, and read Kindle books.

Basic parental controls setup

1. Slide downward via the upper section of the display screen & hit on Settings.
2. Tap Parental Controls

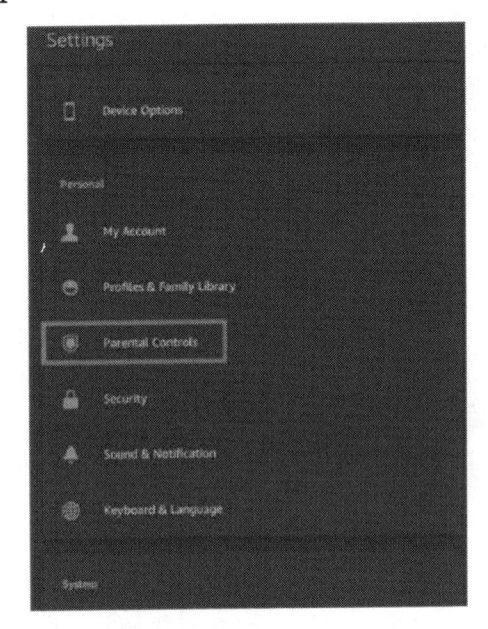

3. Push the Parental Controls toggle.
4. Type in a password and double-check it.
5. Tap Finish.
6. A lock icon will show up at the top of the screen after parental controls have been enabled.

You may choose the content categories you wish to filter from here. Additional apps, websites, and books can be added to an authorized or prohibited list.

Trail these procedures to access the time restrictions and purchase approval settings:

1. Hit on "Parental Controls" via the core settings menu
2. To see or check out the parental controls section, input your passcode
3. Hit on **Time Limits** or **Purchase Approvals** here
4. Via this point, you will be able to choose the limitations you want for each option.

Utilizing Amazon Kids+ to set parental controls

Additionally, it enables parents to establish precise parental restrictions for a child's account. Setting time restrictions, content screening, and purchase approval settings are all included in this.

Follow these procedures to gain access to these features:

1. Switch on the Amazon Fire Max gadget, then slide downward via the upper section of the display screen to input **Settings**. Slide downward the display screen via the upper & hit on Settings.
2. Pick and hit on **Profiles & Family Library** via the "Settings" menu.

3. If your teen or child has a profile, hit on it. If not, make your child's profile on the gadget a new one.
4. On the profile, you may select to subscribe to Amazon Kids+. There are many subscription plans for the service.
5. Access or enter the Amazon Appstore & download the Amazon Kids+ application. This will be utilized to manage your kid's content on the gadget.
6. Launch the Amazon Kids+ application & log in via your Amazon credentials. Then hit on the profile linked with the subscription.

Manage your kid's or teen's profile

Each child profile has a wide range of choices that offer you great control over what they can and cannot do.

1. Select the kid profile you want to manage by going to Settings > Profiles & Family Library.

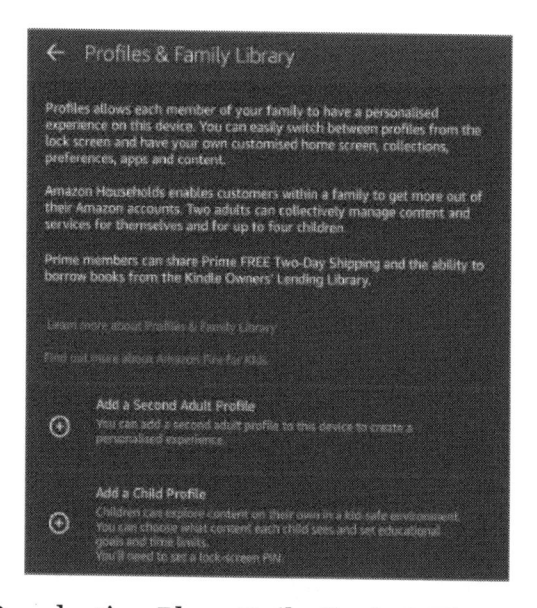

2. By selecting Place Daily Goals & Time limitations, you may block your child from using the tablet at night, place limitations on Total Screen Time, or segment your restrictions by kind of material. For instance, some parents would be OK to let limitless gaming but limit app usage to 30 minutes daily. A notice notifying your kid that they have used all the allotted time for the day appears on the screen when the time restriction is reached. For the weekend in comparison to the week, you might establish various time constraints and restrictions. You may also establish educational objectives, such as mandating that your child read a book for 30 minutes before they can access entertainment materials. You may also establish educational objectives, such as mandating that your child read a book for 30

minutes before they can access entertainment materials.

Under Manage Your Child's material, you may add or remove access to any particular material. You must sign into your profile to download new apps or games for them. Once the apps are downloaded and installed, go to Settings > Profiles & Family Library, choose their profile, press Add Content > Add Books, Videos, And Apps, select the apps or games you want to add, and then hit Done. The age-appropriate recommendations can be overridden if you wish to allow access to any of the content.

3. You will be able to decide if your child can access the web browser on their profile under Web Settings. You can only allow your child to access web content that has been pre-approved depending on their age, known as Amazon Curated Content.

Additionally, you may decide to limit your child's profile's access to the camera and gallery. Any images kids capture won't be uploaded to social media or sent through email, but you may decide to back them up to Amazon Drive automatically if you want to. Make sure the Enable In-App Purchasing option is toggled off to prevent any unanticipated fees or micro-transactions.

How to decide when your child may use their tablet and establish a curfew

1. To activate this function, first hit on the switch after Setting a Curfew.
2. Click Curfew Schedule.
3. Decide which days and hours the youngster won't be permitted to use the gadget.
4. You must input your parental controls password to unlock a device during curfew.

Monitor or keep an eye on your kid's tablet use

1. To keep an eye on your child's Amazon Fire usage, toggle the option next to Monitor This Profile.
2. A parent and kid symbol will be shown at the top of the screen on a monitored profile.
3. To view the data, go to Activity Centre under the Manage Your Content and Devices window's Your Devices page.

You may check out how much time your child has spent using different applications, the books they've read, and the websites they've visited.

Using Amazon FreeTime Unlimited to purchase parental controls

Also provides extra parental control choices, such as preventing your child from accessing certain kinds of information until they've accomplished daily objectives. (i.e., math problems, reading) and shutting itself down at the designated curfew.

Subscribing to Amazon FreeTime Unlimited on an Amazon Fire

1. Slide downward via the upper section of the display screen & click on the Settings icon.
2. Press the Profiles & Family Library knob.
3. Hit on the profile of your teen.
4. Click FreeTime Unlimited to sign up.
5. Select a monthly subscription plan:

Plan for a single child, $4.99 per month (or $2.99 for Prime subscribers): If just one kid in your family is signed up for Amazon FreeTime, or if you only wish to provide one child's profile access to Kindle FreeTime Unlimited,

Family Plan ($9.99 monthly or $6.99 monthly for Prime members, or $119 annually or $83 annually): If your membership is to cover up to four kids living in your home

Using Amazon FreeTime Unlimited's parental controls

1. Tap the FreeTime app.
2. Click the child's profile icon.
3. Select Set Daily Goals & Time Limits and change the toggles to decide how much time they may spend each day (on the smartphone overall) in a particular app.
4. Choose a Turn off by time to prevent them from using their tablet after bedtime.
5. To specify the minimum and maximum ages for the material types they are permitted to see,

hit on Manage your teen's content, followed by Smart Filters.

Disable Parental Controls on your Fire max

1. Slide downward via the upper of the tab display screen. Go to "Settings."
2. Choose "Parental Controls" under "Personal" in the drop-down menu.
3. To utilize Parental Controls, input your passcode & hit on "OK."
4. Switch off the slider next to "Parental Controls."

CHAPTER 11

Screen or display time

1. Hit on the Amazon Kids application
2. Click "Set Daily Goals & Time Limits" after choosing the child whose profile access you wish to limit. To activate settings for your child, tap the toggle.

Setting bedtime up on your gadget

Set the Bedtime feature by

- Deciding to set daily goals and time restrictions
- Choosing a Turn off by the time

Create goals

Encourage your teen & youngster by establishing academic objectives. You may choose how much time your child should spend on each category on the profile settings page, and you can ask them to finish reading and math exercises before playing games.

Using Smart Filters

This setting guarantees that kids will only see material that has been deemed appropriate for the age group you choose.

1. Set the minimum and maximum ages for the stuff your kid will view by selecting "Smart Filters" in the child profile settings' "Manage your Child's Content" section.

Manage your children's screen time on their fire max gadget

Here's how to establish a daily allowance for your child's tablet use as well as certain periods during the day.

You may set time limitations for different sorts of activities, including games and applications, reading, viewing videos, and more, using the controls. Additionally, they include a Bedtime feature that disables tablet use during the hours you specify for going to bed.

Setting up a kid's account on a Fire Max 11

Each teen who will use the tablet has to have their profile before you can set a screen time limit for them. When you first set up your tablet, you'll be asked to establish a kid profile.

1. Adhere to the on-screen direction to configure it

2. When prompted, enter via your Amazon account. To download apps, even free ones, you must follow these steps.
3. Input the individual's name and birthdate. Additionally, you may press Change next to their profile image; they'll undoubtedly want to select that option.
4. After that, you'll be prompted to establish a screen lock since you need to prevent your children from accessing your adult profile to have unfettered access to everything.

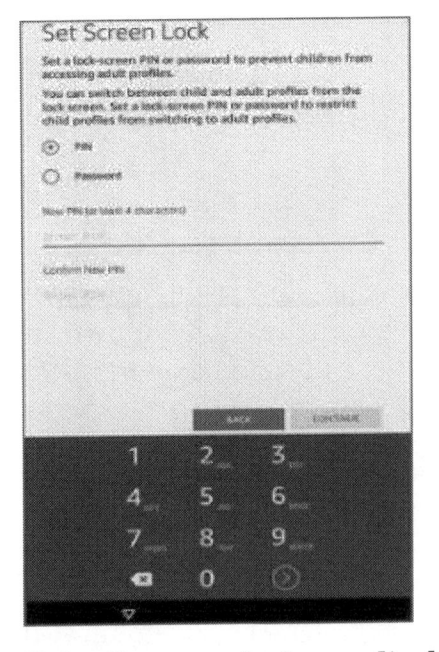

5. You will finally get to the home display after scrolling over calls to download free applications & games & offers of free trials for other Amazon services.
6. If you didn't create a PIN or password when you first set up your tablet, go to Settings,

select Security & Privacy, select Lock-screen passcode to activate it, and then input your preferred passcode.

Switch from your profile to your child's profile

1. Slide downward via the upper section of the screen, slide down again, and press the person symbol, which is displayed below, to move from your profile to that of your child.

2. The following list of users appears: To access the child's profile, simply hit on or click on their name.

Limiting or restricting the amount of time used on your Fire gadget

1. Access the profile settings for your teen or kid.
2. Slide down twice from the top of the screen to reveal the full notification shade on an adult account (or the worried child's account).
3. To access Settings, tap on the cog symbol in the bottom right corner.

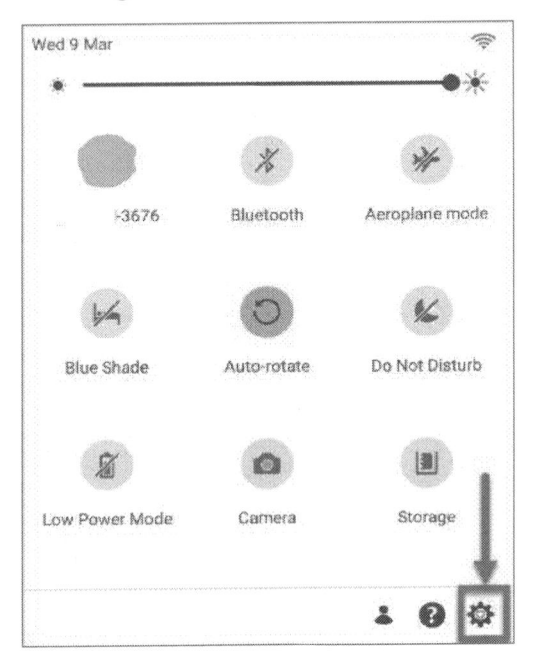

4. (If you try to do this from a kid account, you will need to enter the PIN for an adult account because children cannot access settings.)
5. Select Profiles & Family Library (if you are already logged into a kid profile, you may skip this and the following step).

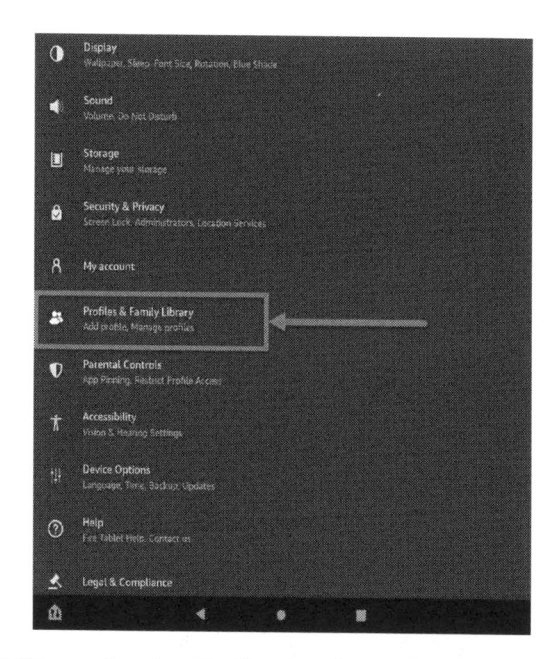

6. Hit on the Set Daily Goals & Time Limits button.

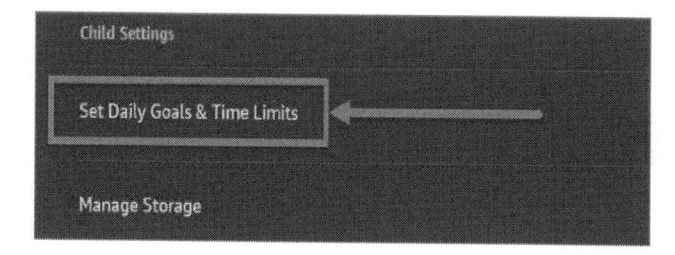

7. Several options, including Bedtime, Goals, and Total Screen Time, will be shown.

Chapter 12

Managing content

Even though Amazon Kids+ has thousands of books, apps, TV series, and movies, each profile may be customized to add or delete items for a specially tailored experience for each kid.

Set language preference

For each kid profile, parents may allow Spanish-only material, English-only content, or a combination of the two.

To set language preferences,
1. Open Amazon Kids Settings and
2. Pick **Language Preferences** under "Manage your child's Content".
3. Choose Spanish, English, or both.

Share the books you've bought with your kid's profile.
1. To choose more applications, films, audiobooks, and other content from your tablet to share with your kid, go to the child profile settings and choose "Manage your Child's Content." Then, choose the "Add Content" option.

Fire on the go

Install your children preferred videos to view when there's the absence of internet service

To use this feature

1. Simply press and hold on to a video to download it to your child's Amazon Kids profile to use this function.
   - When there is no Internet connection, your child may immediately access content that has been downloaded to their Amazon Kids profile.

Deleting paid stuff from your kid's profile

1. In the kid profile settings, select "Manage your Child's Content" and then Just click "Remove Content" and "Remove Unwanted Amazon Kids+ Items." From there you can search by title, and you can locate the titles you wish to restrict using a keyword or content type.

Moving files to your Fire Max gadget

Follow these steps to send files from your PC to your Fire tab:

1. Use a micro-USB cable to connect your Fire Max to your computer (available separately).
2. Slide the arrow from rightward to leftward side to unlock your Max 11.
3. Make sure your computer's Fire Max drive is active. On the computer's desktop, your Fire

Max will show up as an external storage drive or volume. Keep in mind that while your Fire Max 11 is linked to your computer as a storage drive or volume, it cannot be used as a device.
4. Drag and drop your files into the relevant content folder, such as Music or Pictures, as appropriate.
5. Press the Disconnect button at the fire's tab bottom after you're done exchanging files.

Fire the screen, remove it from your computer, unhook the USB wire, and then reattach it.

Erasing or deleting files or content from your Fire max

Delete file or content,

1. Select Remove from Device from the contextual menu that appears when you press and hold on an item.
    - Amazon will continue to store any content you purchase there.

Save it in the cloud for the future

CHAPTER 13

Learn to use the web browser on your fire max 11

You might be startled to learn that there is just one web browser available if you buy an Amazon Fire tablet: Silk.

Amazon's main web browser of choice is Silk. It has a contemporary interface, quick online surfing, and all the features you'd expect from a modern web browser.

Amazon Kids web browser

For your kids, choose the best experience,

1. Go to "Web Settings" and
2. Select "Modify Web Browser."
3. Under Restrict Websites, you will also be able to ban particular websites from there. Go to your child's device settings and select "Add Content" to give them access to more websites and online videos.

Open/Access Browser

1. Scroll through your tablet's programs until you find the Silk Browser, then click it to open the Amazon Fire tablet's browser.
2. To open the browser, hit on this symbol. Like with other browsers, the top of this one has tabs, followed by a URL box and a search field.
3. Via the lower section of this page, you'll see a link that says **Page Settings**. If you choose

that, a choice allowing you to activate or disable the search area above the page's fast links will appear.

Bookmarks

1. To access your list of bookmarks, hit on the Bookmarks knob or button in the menu. You will be able to categorize your bookmarks into subfolders if you'd like.
   - If you're using Silk for the first time and accessing bookmarks, you'll see a button to import your Chrome bookmarks.
   - To finish this, you'll need to carry out a few tasks on a separate computer or mobile device.

To do this, you'll need to carry out a few actions on a separate computer or mobile device.

You will have to open Chrome in a different location and install the Silk Bookmarks browser plugin.

1. To begin, launch the Silk Bookmarks addon
2. Input your Amazon login details
3. Close the extension, reopen it, and choose Import.
4. Lastly, return to the bookmarks page by opening the Silk browser on your tablet. Select Import from Chrome from the menu that appears when you hit on the 3 dots in the upper right angle of the screen.

Reading List

The Reading List is also located in the right menu. If you tap it, two choices will appear:

1. Add the URL to your collection of items you want to read later by clicking **Save to Reading List**
2. View Reading List: Check out the articles on your list of things to read.
    - You may view every page you've added by choosing View Reading List. Since they are color-coded, it's simple to tell which ones you've already read.
    - If it hasn't been read, the title will be orange.
    - Each title will become dark as you read it.

Silk Browser Left Menu

All of the options that were there in the right menu are the same if you choose the left menu icon. There is one exception. The settings will be seen or displayed here.

You may customize every aspect of the Silk browser configuration from the main settings menu.

These include:

- Payment options: save credit cards in your browser for one-click purchases online;
- Passwords: enable automatic password saving and website sign-in;

- Addresses: store addresses in your browser for auto-filling web forms;
- Accessibility: If you have trouble seeing small print, increase the browser's font size and zoom.
- Silk Home: You may customize the Home, Amazon, and News tabs in Silk Home.

The most important step is to personalize your News tab. By controlling your news sources and providers, you may customize the kind of stories and trending news you view.

You may see a list of all the news sources that are accessible on the sources page. Selecting Block will exclude everyone you don't want to be included.

You may enable Do Not Track and Use Secure DNS under the Privacy option to increase your privacy and security.

You must have a provider on hand and enable this setting in the Silk browser if you decide to utilize an encrypted DNS.

You may alter the Silk browser's default search engine using the Advanced options menu.

Select the search engine you wish to use as your default by selecting it from the Advanced options menu..

Reading View and Sharing

This full-screen view is designed to eliminate any outside distractions and give you complete attention to the material you're reading.

- You'll notice Show in Reading View at the bottom of the browser page when Reading View is activated in Setup. Tap it to switch to reading mode.
- As soon as you do this, the entire screen will change, and the content will be formatted more like a typical magazine article.

Switching profile

You should learn how to move between the many accounts you made so that each Amazon Kids user gets material that is appropriate for their age.

Signing in or Authenticating during app startup

1. Access the Amazon Kids app
2. You will be able to choose the profile icon you wish to use to log in by tapping the icon.

Utilizing the lock screen to log in

1. The device's default unlock button will reveal a row of profile icons that are ready for login. Press the profile you wish to enter into, type a password (if one has been set up), and then press Next to access activities in Amazon Kids.

Switching from Amazon Kids

1. Slide downward via the upper section of the display screen &
2. Hit on the **Exit Profile** to move to the lock screen.

Creating passwords
1. Under the "General Settings"
2. Header,
3. To configure this, choose "Enable Child's Lock Screen Password".

CHAPTER 14

Create a Fingerprint, PIN, or Password, or use your Fire Max 11 to sign in.

Instead of a PIN or Passcode, use your fingerprint to unlock your Fire Max 11.

Note: Child profiles do not support fingerprint ID.

1. Open the Settings.
2. Secondly, click Security & Privacy.
3. Choose Fingerprint Unlock
4. Type in your password or PIN
5. Hit on the plus, then adhere to the instructions that appear on the screen.

Each adult profile may register up to five fingerprints.

Using your Fire Max gadget to modify the Pin code or passcode for the lock screen

Have you forgotten your parental controls PIN or lock screen password? Directly from your device's lock screen, reset it.

Your GADGET must be online to change your lock screen passcode or PINCODE

1. Make five incorrect password or PIN entries from the lock screen of your Fire tablet
2. From the screen notice, select Reset Your PIN

3. Type in your Amazon password, then choose Continue
4. Type a fresh PIN or password and then hit Finish.

Unlock your Amazon Fire 11 max

1. Slide the dart icon on the display touch screen from rightward to leftward.

CHAPTER 15

Setting ups on your fire tablet 11

Modify the Fire Tablet's Screen Brightness

By altering the screen brightness on your tablet, you can adapt to changes in your surroundings.

1. From the Settings menu, choose Display
2. Choose Brightness Level, then use the slider to change the brightness of your screen.

Change the Fire Tablet's screen's timeout setting.

By limiting how long your screen is on while not in use, you can conserve battery.

1. In the Settings menu, choose Display or Display & Sounds
2. Next, decide between Sleep or Display
3. Decide how long your screen remains on when not in use, in seconds or minutes.

Adjusting the volume control on your fire max

Use the physical volume knobs on your gadget

- By going to Sound or Sound & Notification in Settings and using the volume slider, you may change the volume.

Mirror your Screen on Your Fire Max 11

On suitable Miracast-enabled devices, display the screen and audio from your Fire tablet (FOS 8 and above).

Make sure your Miracast-capable device is on and discoverable before you mirror the screen of your Fire tablet. For further information, consult the device's user manual.

1. Slide downward via the upper section of the display screen on your Fire gadget
2. From the Quick Settings menu, choose Screen Mirroring
- Screen Mirroring may be found under Connected Devices in Settings.
3. Tap the device name that has Miracast support. It can take up to 20 secs for the link to be formed.
4. Drag downward via upper section of the screen & pick Screen Mirroring once again to shut off the display.

Setting Your Fire Tablet's Time or Clock

Your device's local time setting might help you avoid problems while registering the device.

1. Join a Wi-Fi network using your device.
2. Choose All Options> Device Options > Date & Time from the Home screen
3. Make sure your local time is shown by checking the device's time in the upper-right corner of the screen
4. Disable the Automatic Time Zone setting
5. Allow the choice Automatic time zone back again after waiting five seconds
6. Verify that the device's time shows your local time by checking the time.

Restart your device and attempt these steps again if the time didn't change correctly, or choose your time zone manually.

Pairing your Fire tablet with a PC

Do you wish to access and copy files from a computer to a Fire Max or the other way around? After connecting your device, you may easily download any pictures taken with your tablet onto a Windows or Mac computer. Between the two devices, you may also transfer data like ebooks, music, movies, and other sorts of material.

This article's instructions show you how to connect your Fire Max to a Windows or Mac computer and how to resolve connection problems.

Pair your Amazon gadget with a cable.
1. Hit on "USB preferences" via the Settings menu
2. Hit on **File Transfer** via **the USB for** the segment
3. Select "Internal Storage" and open it. Drag and drag files to the fire tab folder from your PC.

To transfer files from your fire tab, drag & drop them from the "Internal Storage" folder onto your desktop.

First Method

Linking to Windows gadgets
1. Utilize a micro-USB cable to connect the Fire Max to your computer. This is the cord that was included with your gadget. You must order a cord or usb if you don't already possess one.
    - Verify that your Fire max is turned on.
    - This approach may be used to configure a Fire as well.
2. Get your Fire Max unlocked. You may accomplish this by moving the touch screen's arrow from right to left
3. Watch for the Fire max to be detected by your computer. You'll see a pop-up window with choices for controlling the fire max device.
4. **Launch the archive** to see files should be tapped on. Your Fire's data and files will be shown to you in a new File Explorer folder that will open.
    - If this pop-up is absent, launch Windows Explorer by clicking the symbol in the Task Bar that resembles a

folder. Then choose "Computer" in the left-hand sidebar or Kindle or Fire underneath "My Computer".
5. Start your Fire's Settings application. Typically, this may be found under the Utilities folder.
    o You must modify your Fire's file transfer settings in contrast to connecting it to a TV. Your computer might not recognize your Fire Max if this option isn't turned on.
6. Type "USB preferences" into the search box. Additionally, by manually scrolling down, you may look for the USB settings
7. Select the USB Preferences icon. It will launch a fresh page
8. Tap the icon for file transmission. This may be found underneath the USB header.
    o Make sure the circle next to the File transfer is filled in.
9. Open your computer's Internal Storage archive. This is where you may store files on your device and is found under the Fire folder.
10. Insert files by dragging them into the "Internal Storage" folder. Utilize File Explorer to find files from various locations on your PC. Press & hold the file to drop it into the Internal Storage archive.
    o As a consequence, the files will synchronize to your Fire tab.
    o To transfer files from your Kindle Fire to your PC, choose them from the Internal Storage folder and drag them there.
11. Remove the Fire Max from the computer. The Internal Storage folder's top menu will change

to Eject when clicked. Eject can also be selected by right-clicking the device in the File Explorer folder on the left.
By doing this, you may securely unplug your Fire from your computer.
12. Take the Fire's micro-USB cord off of it. It will be possible to utilize the transferred folders

Method 2

Pairing to a Mac

1. On your Mac computer, download the Android File Transfer program. To transfer files from Android to Mac and vice versa, you need this program
2. Use a micro-USB cable to connect the Fire to your Mac computer. You'll need to buy an adaptor if your Mac doesn't have the appropriate port
3. An arrow on the Fire's screen may be shifted from right to left. This unlocks your Fire.
4. Watch for the Fire to be detected by your Mac computer. On your Mac's desktop, a "Fire" or "Fire" icon will show up
5. On your desktop, click the Kindle or Fire icon. The Fire's folders and files are seen in The Finder as a result.
6. Get your Fire's Settings application opened. Typically, this may be found under the Utilities folder
    - The file transfer settings on your Fire will need to be changed. Your computer might not recognize your Fire Max if this option isn't turned on.

7. "USB preferences" should be typed into the search field. Additionally, by manually scrolling down, you may look for the USB settings
8. Select the USB Preferences icon. Another page will be opened
9. Click the icon for file transmission. This is located beneath the Use USB for header
    - Make sure the circle next to the File transfer is filled in.
10. Launch the **Internal Storage** file on your **PC**. This is where you may store files on your device and is found under the fire folder
11. To add the media files to your Fire, drag and drop them. Using the Finder, you may drag and drop your preferred files from your PC to the Fire max.
    - Press & hold the file to drop it into the Internal Storage archive.
    - As a consequence, the files will sync to your Fire Max.
    - To transfer files from your Kindle Fire to your PC, choose them from the Internal Storage folder and drag them there.
12. Removing the Fire Max from the PC.
    - To do this, drag the fire symbol from your desktop to the trash icon in the Dock. The "Eject" symbol appears in place of the trashcan icon
        - Choose Internal Storage as an alternative. In the top menu, select File, then Eject. Alternatively, you may choose the fire's name and the Eject button in the Finder sidebar. This has a

line beneath what seems to be an up arrow
    - You may safely unplug your Kindle Fire via your PC by following this.
13. Take your Fire's micro-USB cable off of it. Your Fire can now be used.

Guide to Troubleshooting fire max 11 won't connect to other devices

1. Connect your Fire Max once again
2. Switch off your Fire Max
3. Close all open applications
4. Update your driver software
5. Updating the fire Max desktop application
6. Install the MTP USB driver
7. Use the camera on your Fire.

CHAPTER 16

The camera on fire max

Usage guide for the camera on Fire max

1. From the home screen, open the Camera app. You can:
2. Tap the screen to concentrate on a particular location inside the Camera app
3. To zoom in or out, use two fingers to squeeze or stretch the screen or the volume controls on the tablet's side.

Fixing your Tablet's Camera

To get your Fire tablet's camera working once again, follow these steps:

1. Start your Fire tablet again
2. Delete any app cache
3. Verify an app's permissions. If a particular app is giving you difficulties, navigate to Settings > Apps & Notifications > App Permissions > Camera, then tap the toggle next to the app to grant it access to the camera. Restart the application, then accept the request for access to the camera when presented
4. Modify the child safety measures. Go to Settings > Parental Controls > Amazon Content and Applications > Camera and toggle it via prohibited to permitted.

5. Install the app again
6. You should swap out the camera of the Fire tablet. If you're feeling tech-savvy and certain that the camera is damaged, you may try changing it yourself
7. Your Fire tablet should be reset. Resetting the tablet will return it to its default settings. Everything you downloaded will be lost, but you may download applications and books again
8. Speak with Amazon for help. You might be able to get your Fire tablet fixed for free if your gadget is still covered under warranty.

CHAPTER 17

Troubleshooting your fire max 11

The most typical Amazon Fire issues and solutions

The Fire tablet won't charge

Your device should not be connected to any charging devices, including the cable and power adapter.

Remove the tablet if you're using a wireless charging dock or mat. Hold the power knob down continuously for 40 secs and then restart your gadget.

Reconnect your device so that it can recharge; connect the power adapter's wire to your device and then plug the outlet adapter into the wall.

While charging, the orange indicator light on your Fire tablet changes. To fix a broken battery or charge port, you may need to mail your tablet in for service or take it to a local independent repair shop if you're still experiencing issues.

Tablet freezing

A soft reset is generally your best option if you discover that your iPad is unresponsive or frozen.

1. merely press down the power knob for 40 secs to restart your gadget. If your tablet is functioning strangely, is unresponsive, or is operating slowly, try this.

Wi-Fi won't work on the Fire

If your Amazon Fire tablet won't connect to WiFi, you can attempt a few troubleshooting methods.

Solutions:

1. To begin with, ensure that the airplane mode was not unintentionally left on.
2. Validate that your Wi-Fi connection is operational and functioning. Make sure that your Wi-Fi connection is live and working. To ensure that your internet is operational, test it with a different device.
3. You can attempt a soft reset by pressing and holding the power knob for 40 secs, or until your gadget restarts.
4. Reset your router or modem. Try reconnecting from the tablet after letting your modem and router restart.

Significant battery drain

Try these solutions if your battery suddenly and unexplainably drains:

Solutions:

1. Press & hold the Power knob for at least 40 secs to restart your gadget. Then, check to see whether it functions normally.
2. One of the programs you've installed likely causes the problem.

You might try deleting applications one at a time while trying to see if you can identify the offending program by going to Settings > Applications & Games

> Manage All Applications. You might also perform a factory reset on the smartphone and install applications only when necessary, keeping an eye out for any changes in battery life. If you do choose to factory reset your tablet, be careful to back up any important files or images beforehand because doing so will erase everything on it. Then, navigate to Settings > Device Options > Reset to Factory Defaults.

Also

1. Make it a practice of shutting off your gadget when not utilized. Once the Power Off box appears, hold down the power button and choose OK.
2. Pull down the notification shade and press to activate Aeroplane mode if you don't want to turn off the device while you aren't using it. You may also select Automatic Smart Suspend under Settings > Power.
3. Low Power Mode, located in Settings > Power, is another option for getting more battery life out of your Fire tablet, but it may darken your display. Additionally, it may be set up to turn on automatically.

E or Digital-books disappearing or not functioning properly

After restarting their tablet, it looks like some customers lose the downloaded e-books, while others find that they don't function offline.

Several approaches exist for this.

1. This issue can be caused by the Google Play Store if you have it set up on your Fire Max gadget. Launch the Play Store application, check out the fire max application page, & choose Uninstall. Return to the Play Store's home page now, press the three vertical lines in the top left, scroll down to Settings, choose Auto-update applications, and then hit Do not auto-update apps. You may still manually update apps by going to the Play Store, clicking the three vertical lines in the top left corner, choosing My Apps & Games, and then clicking the Updates option. Avoid upgrading any Kindle, fire or Amazon applications here; instead, tap Update next to each app you wish to update.
2. whether you don't have access to Google Play Store, try synchronizing your books before pressing and holding the Power button for at least 40 seconds to force a restart, then check to see whether everything is working correctly.
3. You might also try looking for the fire app under Settings > Apps & Games > Manage All

Applications. After pressing Force Stop, clear the cache.

Micro SD card not functioning or not being recognized

Is your micro SD card not being recognized by your Fire tablets? Content on the micro SD card can lose access permanently or only sometimes.

1. Charge your Fire tablet completely using the original cord and charger, and then do a force reset by holding down the Power button for 40 seconds. Join a Wi-Fi network, then let your tablet alone for a time; it should begin downloading and installing any available updates. On your desktop computer or laptop, you may manually complete this task by going to Amazon's website for Fire & Software Updates.
2. Switch off your tablet and take out the micro SD card. Replacing it carefully after that, try once more.
3. Try taking off your tablet's case if it's in one. Pushing on the card can, inadvertently, be the cause of the issue.
4. On your PC, visit the Manage Your Content & Gadget page on Amazon & register yourself. Verify that your device is registered by looking at the listed devices. On your Fire Max, you can also confirm that you're signed up by sliding down from the top of the screen and selecting Settings > My Account > Register. It would also be worthwhile to attempt deregistering; after

restarting your device, you can register once again.
5. You might attempt switching various content categories under Settings > Storage > SD Card. But for the micro SD card, they ought to be turned on by default.
6. If all else fails, switch off your tablet, take the micro SD card out, and insert it into your PC or desktop. Then back up your data before formatting the card. To choose FAT32 or exFAT as the format, right-click the SD card in Windows and choose Format.

Troubleshoot your Fire Max 11's fingerprint access.

How to proceed if your device's fingerprint ID function breaks down

If you experience issues with fingerprint access:

- After it turns on, try sliding up on the display screen
- Check the tablet's profile to see what it is. Ask the profile owner to sign in and swap profiles if it is not yours.

If your fingerprint doesn't still function:

- To log onto your tablet, use your PIN or password.
- Launch Settings
- Opt for Security & Privacy
- Opt for Fingerprint Unlock
- Type your pass code or Pin code all over again.

- To remove already-created fingerprints, tap the trash can symbol.
- To replicate your fingerprint, use the plus button

Installing Google Play Store on your Fire Max

1. Enable Apps From Outside Sources
    - Four APK (Android Package) files must be installed for Google Play to function. The "APK" abbreviation stands for the .apk file extension. As .apk files, Android applications are all bundled. You can't see this portion on the different app shops. However, downloading once you hit Install in the application store, an apk file is downloaded. The Silk web browser can download these files from Amazon; however, Silk cannot perform an automated installation apk files.
    - Launch the Settings program, choose Security & Privacy, then Apps From Unknown Sources, then Silk Browser, to modify that. then switch to the "allow" position. You are now prepared to download files after finishing that.
2. Installing the Application
    - The Google Play Store requires the download of four programs: Google Account Manager, Google Services Framework, Google Play Service, and Google Play Store.

- Store app requires the first three to operate as frameworks, thus they must be installed before the last one.
- At this point, things start to become a bit complex. Different Android versions require distinct installation files since different Android versions are supported depending on the Fire tablet you have. Go to Settings > Device Options > About Fire Tablet to learn which tablet you have.
- All of these files may be downloaded at APKMirror.com. The Google Play Store will update and maintain these applications once they have been acquired & installed via Google's servers. This all indicates that the technique is typically safe.

Here is the application link you are required to download shows. For the time being, download them and do not open them.

3. Download the applications
   - You must now set up the applications. The ideal order must be trailed. Do not press open after you are finished. Before you access the Play Store, we need to reboot. When installing files, they are installed in the following order:

com.google.gsf.login

com.google.android.gsf

com.google.android.gms

com. android.vending

- Restarting your Fire tablet is necessary after installing all four apps. Hit on Restart after holding down the power button until the Power menu appears.
4. Authenticate or go into your Google Account.
    - You ought to be able to access the Google Play Store once your Fire tablet has rebooted, register with your Google Account, & start installing applications. Again, not all of them work, but there is undoubtedly a greater selection here than on Amazon's Appstore

Advanced Options

You can take things a step further and get rid of the Amazon software you don't want if you feel confident utilizing the command line. The Android Debug Bridge is a piece of software that must be installed to accomplish that. The word "Bridge" refers to the developer tool provided by Google that enables PC-based Android tablet interaction. The Debug Bridge's most recent version is available through Google. Once it has been installed, you may use the PC's terminal to execute Android instructions on your Fire tablet.

Before connecting to your tablet, debugging must be enabled. Go to Settings > Device Options > About Fire Tablet, press the serial number seven times, and you're done. Return to Device Options and scroll down until Developer Options appears as a new menu option. Turn on Developer choices, then click the USB

Debugging toggle switch after moving down the list of choices to find it.

Now you may use Android Debug Bridge, often known as adb, to connect to your tablet. Open a terminal window & input adb gadgets to accomplish it. A Fire device should have the word "unauthorised" alongside it on the list. It's alright; simply check your Fire tablet for a notice asking whether you want to enable USB debugging. Select Yes, then return to your PC and enter adb devices once more. After your device, it should now simply say "device" rather than "unauthorized". You may now use your computer to carry out commands.

Rooting a Fire Max

For access to more functions, root your Fire Max.

1. To access your settings on your Fire max, scroll downward via the upper section of the screen & hit on gear symbol.
2. Tap Device Options.
3. Continue tapping the Serial Number box until Developer Options show beneath it
4. Tap Developer Options
5. Click Enable ADB to launch Android Debug Bridge.
6. Re-tap "activate"
7. Return to Setups & select Security & Privacy.
8. To enable the installation of program via sources other than the Amazon store, hit on program via Unknown Sources.
9. Utilize a USB connection to link your Fire tablet to your PC.

10. Download the Amazon Fire Utility to your PC from the XDA developer forums.
11. Take the Fire Utility ZIP folder's contents and move them to your desktop or another location on your computer.
12. HIT on the Windows Batch (.bat) file twice to launch the Fire Utility.
13. Input the no of the activity you intend performing & hit on Enter
14. The instructions that are displayed should be Followed
15. Exit the Fire Utility, then unplug your tablet from your computer. Your device might need to restart or go through a factory reset for changes to take effect.

Made in the USA
Columbia, SC
19 March 2025